White Rock Christian Academy
2265 - 152nd Street
Surrey, B.C. V4A 4P1

AIDS ISSUES

A Handbook

DAVID E. NEWTON

—Issues in Focus—

ENSLOW PUBLISHERS INC.

Bloy Street & Ramsey Ave.
Box 777
Hillside, N.J. 07205
U.S.A.

P.O. Box 38
Aldershot
Hants GU12 6BP
U.K.

This book is dedicated to

Ruth Brinker and the volunteers at Open Hand

as representatives

of the countless men and women working in AIDS organizations

throughout the nation and the world

Library of Congress Cataloging-in-Publication Data

Newton, David E.
    AIDS issues: a handbook / David E. Newton.
        p. cm.—(Issues in focus)
    Includes index.
    Summary: Discusses current medical, social, and political issues concerning HIV and the AIDS virus.
    ISBN 0-89490-338-1
    1. AIDS (Disease)—Social aspects—Juvenile literature. [1. AIDS (Disease) 2. HIV infections.] I. Title. II. Series: Issues in focus (Hillside, N.J.)
RC607.A26N49 1992
362.1'969792—dc20   92-10071
                                                 CIP
                                                  AC

Printed in the United States of America

10 9 8 7 6 5 4 3 2 1

Cover Photo: PhotoEdit.

AIDS ISSUES
A Handbook

I. BACKGROUND OF THE AIDS EPIDEMIC

II. THE ISSUES

7 AIDS AND HEALTH WORKERS 77

8 EDUCATION TO STOP THE EPIDEMIC 87

I
BACKGROUND OF
THE AIDS EPIDEMIC

1

Issues Concerning AIDS

Hundreds of books about AIDS (acquired immunodeficiency syndrome) have now been written. Many of these books provide accurate scientific information about the disease. Others explain how to avoid the infection that leads to AIDS or how to live a productive life if and when one does become infected. Still other books describe the personal experiences of people who have contracted AIDS.

This book has a different purpose. It discusses some of the social, political, economic, ethical, and other issues that have arisen as a result of the AIDS epidemic.

When we talk about an issue, we usually mean a topic about which people hold a variety of opinions. For example, the question has been raised as to whether all medical workers ought to be tested for the virus that causes AIDS (HIV—human immunodeficiency virus). Some people say yes, others say no, and still others say sometimes yes, sometimes no.

In most cases, there is a lot of factual information available on these topics. For example, scientists know a great deal about the way in which HIV is transmitted. That information is readily available to people who want to have it.

We might wish that people would always agree on the right course of action, based on the best available information. If that happened, there might well be fewer issues involving the AIDS epidemic.

But that does not happen often, for at least two reasons. In the first place, people may not always agree about the facts of an issue, and facts all by themselves do not necessarily lead to a correct decision. People use and interpret facts in terms of their own religious and moral background and their philosophies of life.

What does it mean, for example, to know that the chance of being infected by a medical worker is about 1 in 300,000? Different people will interpret that information in different ways. Some will say the risk is so low as to be negligible. Others will say that any risk is too large.

In the second place, people make decisions with more than their minds. They also act on the basis of emotions, such as fear and hatred. You may or may not agree that basing decision on emotions is good. But it happens.

What this means is that issues involving the AIDS epidemic often have no simple correct answer. People of goodwill, working with the same set of facts, can disagree about testing, the use of test results, funding for AIDS research, the best form of education on AIDS, and so on.

Unlike other books on the AIDS epidemic, this one will not try to convince you what is right or wrong about various AIDS-related issues. Instead, it will try to present and explain the variety of attitudes that people have about these issues. You may believe that some people hold attitudes on certain issues that are illogical or insensitive. Of course, you are entitled to your opinion.

But the fact remains that differences of opinion do exist on these issues. Groups of people strongly believe in one or another of the arguments presented on these issues. Our position is that everyone should be informed about the statements people have made about AIDS-related issues. Then, understanding those positions and knowing the facts about these issues, each person can make up her or his own mind about each of the topics discussed here.

The issues presented in this book are not the only ones that could have been included. But they are typical of the kind of controversies that have arisen as a result of the AIDS epidemic. You may discover other AIDS issues that are more interesting or more important to you.

Also, be aware that issues change over time. Questions that may have been vitally important five years ago may have been resolved. Issues that no one worried about last year may be critically important two years from now. Solutions that made sense in 1989 may no longer be satisfactory in 1999.

The greatest value in this book may be in learning how to think about AIDS issues, not in finding the right answer for any one given issue. The book is laid out in a way to help you develop this skill. You should begin by reading all of Part I of the book. Part I provides scientific and historical background on the AIDS epidemic. It also describes a typical AIDS issue that involves schools and students. The Ryan White story illustrates some of the problems involved in dealing with AIDS issues.

Part II describes some typical controversies involving AIDS. Each section in Part II provides some background information on an issue and outlines the positions that people have taken on that issue. You should read and think about this information and the pros and cons of each question. Then you can decide what you believe about that issue.

2

Kids, AIDS, and Schools

Ryan White did not look very different from most other 13-year old boys. He was friendly, energetic, full of fun . . . a nice kid to be around. He was an honor student at Western Middle School in Kokomo, Indiana. Like many kids his age, he had a paper route after school. And he had a girlfriend.

But Ryan was not like most other teenagers. He was a hemophiliac. A hemophiliac is a person whose body lacks a substance needed to make blood clot. If a hemophiliac is cut or bruised, the bleeding is very difficult to stop.

Today, hemophilia can be controlled. Hemophiliacs can take injections of the clotting substance their bodies lack. They can lead a nearly normal life.

But Ryan was unlike most other teenagers for another reason. He had AIDS.

AIDS is the abbreviation for a disease whose full name is acquired immunodeficiency syndrome. Ryan got AIDS from the injections he took to control his hemophilia.

AIDS is a very frightening disease. No cure for it has been discovered yet. Anyone who gets AIDS is likely to become very ill and may die from the disease.

Most people would never have guessed that Ryan was seriously ill in 1984. True, he did miss a lot of school. But Ryan's schoolmates, friends, and neighbors didn't think too much about that. Besides his mother, only some of the school officials in Kokomo knew that Ryan was ill with AIDS. His mother had told them in order to explain Ryan's many absences from school.

Then, in March 1985, things began to change for Ryan, his family, and the citizens of Kokomo. The local newspaper carried a story about Ryan. It told how he and other hemophiliacs had contracted AIDS during their treatments. What had once been a private secret was now known to everyone in Kokomo.

When summer vacation ended in August of 1985, Ryan was not allowed to reenter school. The school board had decided that it would be in the best interests of everyone if Ryan did not return to school.

Instead, the board suggested some alternatives. It would provide a special tutor who would teach Ryan at home. Or it would arrange a private telephone hook-up between Ryan's home and his classroom. Ryan's mother refused these offers. She insisted that Ryan be readmitted to school. In August of 1985, the Whites filed suit to force the school to enroll Ryan.

By now, however, the Ryan White story had become national news. Actor Rock Hudson had just been diagnosed with AIDS. The national media were beginning to write and talk about this "new and frightening," "terrifying," "deadly, mysterious disease."[1] On August 26, CBS, ABC, and NBC all carried stories about Ryan White. Suddenly, a difficult problem for the town of Kokomo had become a nationwide drama.

Citizens of Kokomo began to take sides on the Ryan White issue. Some parents of Ryan's classmates supported the Whites. The local newspaper wrote a number of editorials arguing that Ryan should be readmitted to school. It collected more than $100,000 for the White family to help pay for Ryan's medical bills.[2]

But some parents were frightened and angry. They did not want their children to have any contact with Ryan. They worried that Ryan would spread AIDS the way a child spreads a cold. They knew that health authorities said that AIDS could not be transmitted very easily. But they could not be certain. What if health authorities were wrong. After all, AIDS was a deadly disease from which no one recovered.[3]

At times the debate became ugly. The Kokomo reporter who wrote about Ryan received death threats and many offensive telephone calls. His house with bombarded with eggs. Even his father attacked him, cutting his arm with a broken bottle.[4]

In April 1986, a federal court in Indianapolis ordered the school board to readmit Ryan. But that victory did not mean very much. Many parents were still angry and worried. They refused to let their children play with Ryan. Ryan explained that "a lot of people would back away from me on the street. They'd run away from me."[5]

Finally, a year later, the Whites decided they had had enough. They were tired of the "hostility and loneliness" from people in their hometown.[6] They moved from Kokomo to a new home in Cicero, Indiana.

The citizens of Cicero appeared more willing to accept Ryan as "just another kid." In 1988 Indiana's governor, Robert Orr, declared a Ryan White Day honoring the brave young man, his family, and his school.

The story of Ryan White does not have a happy ending. In April of 1990, Ryan finally died of AIDS.

Kids with AIDS: Should People Fear Them?

Ryan White's story is not the only case of its kind. In many other instances, children with AIDS have been kept from attending school. In New York City in 1985, for example, three children were banned from schools when officials learned that their mothers had boyfriends who were intravenous drug users.[7]

Another case involved Richard, Robert, and Randy Ray. The three sons of Clifford and Louise Ray were all hemophiliacs. All three of the boys had been infected with the HIV by blood transfusions, but had not developed any symptoms of AIDS. When officials learned that the boys had HIV, they banned them from entering schools in Arcadia, Florida, and Bay Minette, Alabama. When the Ray home was burned down in Arcadia, the family finally moved to Sarasota, Florida, where the boys were enrolled in school with no further problems.

Much more is known about AIDS today than was known in 1985. Yet some parents and school officials still question the advisability of allowing children with AIDS to attend school. Are these concerns legitimate?

These fears are not difficult to understand. Scientists have now made great progress in learning about the disease and in finding ways to treat it. But even today there is no cure. A child who develops AIDS is faced with a very difficult medical problem. We can understand why parents might be concerned about having their children exposed to such a serious health risk.

Parents may wonder about the possible dangers of AIDS transmission at school. For example, think of the rough housing that goes on. Imagine what might happen if two boys—one of whom has AIDS—get into a fight, get cut, and start to bleed? Can we be 100 percent certain, parents ask, that the infected boy would not transmit AIDS to the uninfected boy?

Besides, some people argue, children with AIDS should stay out of school for their own good. These children pick up infections very easily. They would constantly be at risk for measles, mumps, chicken pox, and other diseases.

Given these potential risks, perhaps children with AIDS should be isolated from their classmates. Can't they learn just as well from private home tutors or through closed-circuit television?

Opponents disagree with these arguments. They point out that no child has ever contracted AIDS from another child in school and that the disease cannot be transmitted by touching, by sharing utensils or food, or by being in the same room with an infected person. In fact, studies have been made of the even closer contact among families members. These studies show that none of the family members of more than 14,000 AIDS patients has ever contracted the disease from the person who has AIDS.[8]

Besides, isolating a child from his or her classmates is a terrible thing to do, many people say. The child with AIDS already faces difficult emotional problems with his or her disease. Should the child also be deprived of contact with friends? Even if they can learn as much through tutors or closed-circuit TV, children with AIDS need to spend time with their friends.

Questions have also been raised about teachers who have AIDS. One case involved a third-grade teacher in Marin County, California. At the opening of school in the fall of 1991, the teacher announced that he had AIDS. He was still healthy enough to work, and he wanted to continue teaching. But he knew that some parents and children might be worried.

Therefore, the school board held a meeting at which the teacher described his medical condition. He wanted to educate parents and students about AIDS. He wanted to explain that his students were not at risk for the disease just by being in his class. (Being "at risk" means having a chance of being infected by some disease, in this case, AIDS.)

Most parents were satisfied by the teacher's explanation. They were convinced that he was a good teacher and his health problems were unrelated to his job. They wanted their children to stay in his class.

But other parents were uncertain. They found it difficult to believe that the risk for their children was absolutely zero. No matter what scientists said, they did not want to take any chance at all that the teacher might pass the disease to someone in his class. These parents were allowed to transfer their children to other third-grade classes.

Problems also continue to exist for the parents of children with AIDS. In New York City, for example, many of these parents refuse to let their children attend school because they fear they will be shunned or attacked. They know that the law allows the children to go to school. But they prefer to keep them at home rather than face problems at school.[9]

Ryan's Story Shows AIDS Creates Complicated Issues

Ryan White has become more than just a brave young man in Indiana. Today his story stands for many of the difficult, complicated issues that surround the AIDS epidemic. How can we understand and resolve those issues?

It helps to know that scientists have now learned a great deal of information about AIDS. They know what causes the disease, how it is transmitted, and how to control it.

Many of those facts were known to Ryan, his parents, his schoolmates and teachers, and to those who lived in his town. For example, most people had been told that the chance of catching AIDS from Ryan was very small, probably zero.

But knowing those facts was not enough for many of these people. They were still frightened and worried. They could not help asking, "But what if . . . ?" Some people were so upset that they did terrible things. They may look back some day and say, "How could we have acted that way?"

One answer for this type of question is that some people are not always convinced by the facts they are given. They are not sure that scientists really know all they think they know. More important, in many cases, is the fact that worry and fear can sometimes count for more than knowledge.

And that's the way it is with AIDS issues. The disease can be terribly frightening. People don't always know who and what to believe about the disease. Even when people do know the facts, they often do not act on these facts. They do what makes them feel good or safe or right.

AIDS Issues

Issues involving the AIDS epidemic arise in many parts of our lives. The Ryan White story shows how schools have had to deal with the disease. But so have insurance companies; police officers; doctors, nurses, and dentists; politicians; medical researchers; landlords; corporations and unions; and, of course, the people who have AIDS.

Part II of this book describes in more detail some of the many AIDS-related issues in our society today. However these issues differ from each other, one thing can be said about them all. In order to understand these issues, one must first understand the disease itself. Therefore, the next chapter summarizes some of the most important information scientists have learned about AIDS. The chapter tells about the history of the epidemic, how the disease is caused, how it is transmitted, and what methods are used to control it. Once you have mastered this information, you will be better able to think about and take a position on the issues in Part II.

3

History of The AIDS Epidemic

The doctor was puzzled. The symptoms he saw in front of him were highly unusual. The dark purple blotches on the patient's skin were a sure sign of Kaposi's sarcoma (KS). KS was a very rare disease. It normally occurred only in old men. But this patient was only twenty-five years old! The doctor had never heard of KS in a man this young before. Even more surprising was the fact that this was the third young man with KS he had seen in a month. [1] The year was 1981. The place was New York City. American doctors were getting their first look at a terrible new disease: AIDS.

Within months, doctors in Los Angeles and San Francisco were finding another medical puzzle. They began to see young men who were ill with a rare form of pneumonia called *Pneumocystis carinii pneumonia* (PCP). PCP was sometimes observed in patients undergoing chemotherapy (medical treatment with drugs). But it never occurred in otherwise healthy young men. The young men in New York, Los Angeles, and San Francisco had all been healthy until a few months before they saw their doctors.

Kaposi's sarcoma and PCP were soon recognized as diseases related to AIDS. By the end of 1981, 168 cases of AIDS-related diseases had been reported.

The Epidemic Spreads in the United States

What did these 168 men have in common that could explain how they got this disease? Medical workers found only one thing: All the men were either gay or bisexual. It looked as though AIDS might be transmitted by some form of homosexual activity. Some people began to call the new disease "gay cancer."

Before long, medical workers realized that homosexual activities were not the only way AIDS was transmitted. They began to see injecting drug users who had developed the disease. The term "injecting drug user" refers to people who use needles to inject themselves with drugs. Some injecting drug users inject drugs directly into their blood streams. They are also called intravenous (IV) drug users. Other injecting drug users inject drugs under the skin but not into the blood stream. As an example, some people inject steroids under the skin but not into the bloodstream.

AIDS also showed up in a third group of people, those who had received blood transfusions. The first member of this group to get AIDS was a hemophiliac. Hemophiliacs often require blood transfusions. The first hemophiliac with AIDS was reported in May 1982.

A fourth cluster of AIDS cases occurred among babies whose mothers were injecting drug users. Apparently the babies became infected with the disease before they were born.

AIDS cases can also be transmitted by heterosexual activity. Men can be infected by women, and women can be infected by men. For example, men and women who have unprotected sex with an injecting drug user are at high risk for AIDS. The term "unprotected sex" refers to any sexual activity in which the transmission of body fluids (primarily blood, semen, and vaginal secretions) is not prevented. An example of protected sex is any form of intercourse in which a condom is used. The condom is designed to prevent body fluids from passing between two individuals.

What is High Risk Behavior?

The term "high risk group" is often used in discussions about AIDS. Most often, the term is used to refer to gay and bisexual men and injecting drug users because, in the past, the large majority of AIDS cases occurred among members of these groups.

For at least two reasons, this kind of labeling is wrong and dangerous. First, many people in a "high risk group" are not at risk because they do not engage in risky behavior. For example, many gay and bisexual men no longer engage in unprotected sex. So they are not at risk for the transmission of AIDS.

Second, it is not a person's lifestyle that is risky but a person's behavior. For example, heterosexual married men may sometimes have sexual experiences with other men. These married men probably do not think of themselves as "gay" or even "bisexual." Yet, if they engage in risky behavior, such as anal intercourse without a condom, they are at risk for AIDS.

For these reasons, health authorities agree that the best way to talk about risk for AIDS is in terms of behaviors. Scientists now agree that the agent that causes AIDS can be transmitted by any behavior that involves the sharing of body fluids between two people. For example, two injecting drug users may share a needle with each other. When they do so, the blood of one person may be passed on to the second person. The agent that causes AIDS may be passed on also, along with the blood.

Also, when two people have unprotected sex, semen may be transmitted from one person to another. The agent that causes AIDS may be carried along in the semen.

Trends in the United States

Since 1981 the AIDS epidemic has grown rapidly in the United States. By 1987 at least one case of AIDS had been reported in every state. Officials at the national Centers for Disease Control estimate that at least one million Americans have contracted the agent that causes AIDS.[2]

Figure 1 shows the increase in AIDS cases to date. It also shows the number of people in the United States who have died as a result of AIDS.

The pattern of AIDS cases has begun to change significantly in the last few years. Although the number of new AIDS cases among gay and bisexual men continues to increase, the rate of increase has begun to slow down. In 1990, only half of the new AIDS cases reported involved gay men. New infections among injecting drug users, however, continue to climb at an alarming rate.

AIDS Among Women, Heterosexuals, Minorities, and Children

Health authorities are increasingly concerned about the growth of AIDS cases among women, heterosexuals, and children. Figures 2 through 4 show the patterns of infections among various groups of individuals between 1981 and 1991.

In 1990 women constituted 11.5 percent of all reported cases of AIDS. This fraction is about double the rate for the preceding decade. Just over one-half of the 4,890 women with AIDS in 1990 were blacks. Another one-fifth were Hispanic, and one-fourth were white. Considering the percentage of blacks,

Fig. 1: AIDS Cases and Deaths 1981-1991

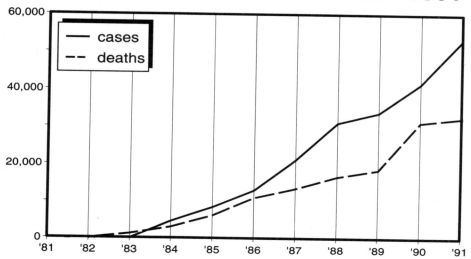

Sources: "Summary of Notifiable Diseases, United States, 1990," *Morbidity and Mortality Weekly Report*, October 4, 1991, Tables 1 and 7; "Mortality Attributable to HIV Infection/AIDS—United States, 1981-1990," *Morbidity and Mortality Weekly Report*, January 25, 1991, p. 41 and Table 1; "The HIV/AIDS Epidemic: The First 10 Years," *Morbidity and Mortality Weekly Report*, June 7, 1991, pp. 357-363+; and "The Second 100,000 Cases of Acquired Immunodeficiency Syndrome—United States, June 1981 - December 1991," *Morbidity and Mortality Weekly Report*, January 17, 1992, page 28.

Fig. 2: Women and AIDS, 1981-1990

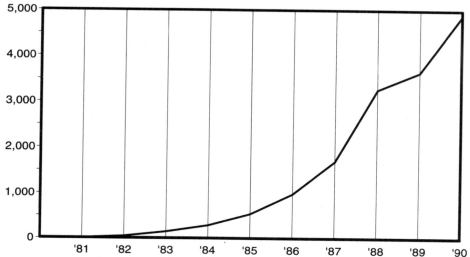

Source: Tedd V. Ellerbrock, Timothy J. Bush, Mary E. Chamberland, and Margaret J. Oxtoby, "Epidemiology of Women With AIDS in the United States, 1981 Through 1990," *JAMA*, June 12, 1991, Table 1.

Hispanics, and whites in the general population, these figures mean that a black woman is thirteen times as likely to be infected as is a white woman, and a Hispanic woman is eight times as likely to be infected as a white woman.

The problem is particularly severe in certain regions of the United States. In some parts of New York City, more than 2 percent of the women of child-bearing age have been infected with the agent that causes AIDS. AIDS is now the leading cause of death among black women of reproductive age (fifteen to forty-four years) in the states of New York and New Jersey.[3]

Infection is an especially serious problem for pregnant women. Studies show that between 25 and 35 percent of infected pregnant women transmit the AIDS agent to their newborn children. As a result, of the approximately 6,000 infants born to infected women in 1989, between 1,500 and 2,000 were also infected.[4]

The rate of AIDS cases among heterosexuals has also increased dramatically. In most cases, heterosexuals contract AIDS from someone who engages in high risk behavior. The sex partners of injecting drug users and bisexuals are also at high risk for infection.

Magic Johnson Announces That He Has The AIDS Virus

The risk of HIV infection among heterosexuals was dramatically illustrated on November 7, 1991. On that date, professional basketball star Earvin "Magic" Johnson announced that he had been infected by HIV. Johnson made it very clear that he had become infected by having heterosexual intercourse with an infected woman. He didn't know exactly who his infected partner had been. But he knew that it was a woman since, as he explained on a national television program, he was "far from being a homosexual." Johnson

Heterosexual Men and AIDS, 1981-1990

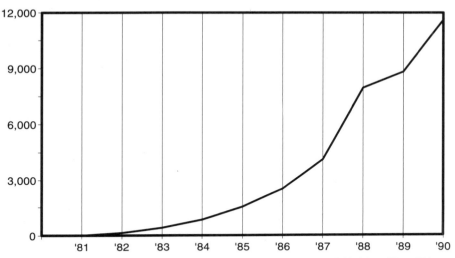

Source: Tedd V. Ellerbrock, Timothy J. Bush, Mary E. Chamberland, and Margaret J. Oxtoby, "Epidemiology of Women With AIDS in the United States, 1981 Through 1990," *JAMA*, June 12, 1991, Table 1.

Children and AIDS, 1982-1990

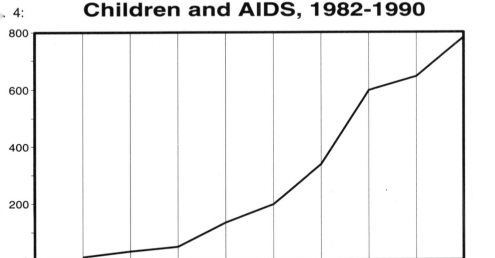

Source: "ACQUIRED IMMUNODEFICIENCY SYNDROME (AIDS)—Pediatric Cases by Year of Report, United States, 1982-1990," in "Summary of Notifiable Disease, United States, 1990," *Morbidity and Mortality Weekly Report*, October 4, 1991, p. 15.

explained that he had been having unprotected sex with many, many women since having become a famous basketball star.

Health authorities praised Johnson for his courage in announcing his HIV status publicly. Johnson immediately became very active in helping educate all Americans about the danger of HIV. Within two weeks, President Bush had appointed him to the President's Commission on AIDS.

But experts also pointed out that Johnson's sexual history illustrated one of the most serious problems in the AIDS epidemic today. Too many heterosexual men and women do not believe that they can become infected with HIV. Even ten years into the epidemic, they continue to practice unprotected sex. The tragic story of Magic Johnson's infection clearly demonstrates how dangerous that assumption can be.

The rate of infection among adolescents also appears to be climbing. The 1988 Presidential Commission on AIDS reported that between 1.5 and 2 percent of teenagers visiting Baltimore health clinics had been infected with the agent that causes AIDS. Department of Defense data showed that one in four hundred teenagers who volunteered for military service was infected. In the District of Columbia, that rate was one in two hundred.

The pattern of infection among adolescents is different in some important ways from the pattern among adults. For example, heterosexual transmission occurs more commonly among teenagers than it does among adults. Also, the infection rate among black and Hispanic teenagers is higher than it is among black and Hispanic adults.[5]

Increases in AIDS in Small Towns and Rural Areas

Yet another trend is the increase in AIDS cases in small towns and rural areas. At one time, AIDS was very much a problem of large cities. To a large extent, it still is. But today, cases of AIDS are growing more rapidly outside of big cities than inside them. Small-town physicians reported 3,803 cases of AIDS in 1989, an increase of 32 percent over 1988. For rural areas, the count was 2,791 AIDS cases, an increase of 37 percent. By comparison, the rate of increase in large urban areas was about 5 percent.[6]

This trend is a source of concern for public health authorities. Generally speaking, hospitals and health care professionals in small towns and rural areas do not have the facilities or the experience to deal with AIDS cases.

The Cause of AIDS: HIV (Human Immunodeficiency Virus)

At first, scientists had no idea how AIDS was caused. Some used names such as gay-related immune deficiency disease (GRID), acquired community immune deficiency syndrome (ACIDS), and community acquired immune deficiency syndrome (CAIDS) to describe the disease.[7] They soon decided that these names were inappropriate. People other than gay men also became ill with the disease. The Centers for Disease Control (CDC) then decided to call the disease acquired immunodeficiency syndrome, or AIDS.[8]

In 1984 scientists discovered the cause of AIDS. A French research team headed by Dr. Luc Montagnier found that the disease was caused by a virus. The same discovery was made at about the same time by an American team lead by Dr. Robert Gallo. The AIDS virus was found to be similar to viruses that cause leukemia in humans and cats. Both French and U.S. researchers gave their own names to the virus, LAV and HTLV-III, respectively. In 1986, the name of the virus was officially changed to human immunodeficiency virus, or HIV.

How HIV Causes AIDS

The way in which HIV causes AIDS is now well understood. It attacks and destroys cells that are part of the immune system. The immune system consists of cells, fluids, and chemicals in the body that protect us against infection.

An important part of the immune system is a type of cell known as the T-helper cell. (These cells are also called T-4 cells.) They become active when bacteria, fungi, viruses, or other foreign materials ("germs") enter the blood stream. The T-helper cells stimulate the immune system to fight against these materials.

When HIV enters the blood stream, it destroys T-helper cells. Without T-helper cells, the immune system does not work properly. Germs that get into the blood stream are not destroyed. Instead, they reproduce and cause an infection.

To visualize the effect of HIV, imagine that cold germs enter a person's body. If the person's body is healthy, the immune system begins to fight back immediately; T-helper cells become active in fighting against the cold germs. Before long, the germs are killed, and the cold infection disappears.

A person whose body contains HIV has a different reaction. His or her immune system is very weak. Very few T-helper cells are present. The cold germs are not killed. They survive, reproduce, and continue to cause infection. A disease that is a simple problem for a healthy person can become a serious concern for someone with HIV infection.

A similar story can be told for many different germs. We are surrounded by millions of disease-causing organisms all the time. For a healthy immune system, these substances are usually no problem. Infections do not occur, or if they do, they clear up quickly.

In a person with HIV infection, any germ can cause a disease that hangs on and on and that may, in some cases, cause death. Infections like these—harmless in healthy bodies but serious in those with HIV—are called opportunistic infections.

A Different Explanation for AIDS

Nearly all scientists today are convinced that AIDS is caused by HIV. But a few scientists hold different views. Probably the most famous dissenter is Dr. Peter Duesberg. Dr. Duesberg is a respected virologist (a scientist who studies viruses) at the University of California at Berkeley.

Dr. Duesberg believes that AIDS is caused not by a virus but by certain types of drugs. He thinks that even one of the drugs used to treat AIDS, AZT (azidothymidine), may actually cause the disease. The way these drugs cause AIDS, according to Dr. Duesberg, is by destroying T-cells and other cells that are part of the immune system.

Dr. Duesberg points to a number of facts about AIDS that suggest the disease is not caused by a virus. For example, most people with AIDS are gay or injecting drug users. No true virus, he says, can be that selective. It would spread beyond such limited groups to the general population.

Also, HIV can take up to ten years to become active in the body. We do not know of any germs that take that long to attack the body, Dr. Duesberg says. In general, Dr. Duesberg refuses to accept most of the data that other scientists agree have proved that HIV is the cause of AIDS.[9]

Many scientists are angry with Dr. Duesberg's position. They point out that he has never done research on HIV. Many are concerned about the message Dr. Duesberg is giving the general public. Dr. William Hazeltine of Harvard University claims that Dr. Duesberg has done damage because of his "serious confusion and misrepresentation of fact." And Dr. Donald Francis at the Centers for Disease Control worries that "when you say HIV does not cause AIDS, don't worry about it, that is dangerous teaching."[10]

It is probably fair to say that almost all scientists who study HIV and AIDS reject Dr. Duesberg's theories. They have no doubt about the role of HIV in causing AIDS.

AIDS-Related Illness

People talk about AIDS is if it was a single disease. But it is not. Instead, HIV causes a number of medical problems, all resulting from the body's failed immune system. For example, an organism called *Candida* occurs commonly on the skin and the mucous membranes of most people. Normally the organism is held under control by the immune system. It causes no serious health problems.

In people with HIV, the immune system cannot provide that control. Instead, *Candida* begins to grow rapidly. It often shows up as a white, yeast-like growth in the mouth, sometimes known as "thrush." The condition is very uncomfortable and may make it difficult for a person to swallow.

Thrush is not fatal and can be treated with drugs. It is an example, however, of one of the many infections that people with HIV may experience, many of which are practically unknown in healthy people. [11]

Another example of an HIV-related infection is mycobacterium avium intracellulare (MAI). This disease is similar to tuberculosis. The bacteria that cause it are common in air and dust. They sometimes infect birds and cause a kind of "bird-tuberculosis." But they almost never survive in a human body.

Only in people who have HIV are these bacteria able to survive, grow, and cause MAI. A number of drugs are available to treat it, but none are very effective. People who develop this disease often die very quickly.

Thrush, MAI, KS, and PCP are only four examples of diseases caused by HIV. A much longer chapter would be needed to tell about all known AIDS-related diseases. Without an effective immune system, a person can develop almost any kind of infection, many of which can be fatal.

What Is Likely to Happen to Someone Who Is Infected with HIV?

It is impossible to say exactly how any one person will respond to HIV. But the general pattern among those with HIV is fairly clear.

The first symptoms of an HIV infection may show up anywhere from a few months to ten years or more after the virus enters the body. Most people might not think much about those symptoms: more colds than usual, loss of weight, heavy sweating at night, and so on.

Eventually, however, those symptoms begin to include more serious problems: thrush, shingles (a painful chicken-pox-like disease), weakness of nerves and muscles, and swelling of the glands, for example. These problems are an early warning that a person's immune system has been damaged.

The words used to described someone who has been infected with HIV change with the progress of the infection. At some point after a person has been infected with HIV, tests will show that infection has occurred. At that point, the person is said to be "HIV positive," "HIV+," or "seropositive." (The prefix sero- refers to serum, a component of blood.) In comparison, a person who has not been infected with HIV is said to be "HIV negative," "HIV-," or "seronegative."

An HIV+ person often shows no signs or symptoms of infection for months or years. Chances are that you see one or more HIV+ people every day.

Later, even more serious diseases begin to appear. KS and PCP are the most common of these. The presence of these diseases is taken as an indication that HIV infection is so bad that the immune system can no longer protect the body. To a doctor, these are "official" signs that a person has contracted full-blown AIDS, also called frank AIDS.

The symptoms and diseases accompanying an HIV infection are much the same for both men and women. One major difference is that women

33

appear to develop KS much less often than do men. For women, PCP is the most common AIDS-related opportunistic infection.[12]

The names we use for people who are infected with HIV are very important. For one thing, medical benefits are usually available for those in one stage of the disease (when they have full-blown AIDS) but not another (when they are first HIV+).

Also, people who are infected care about the names used for themselves. For example, most do not like to be called "victims" of the disease. Probably the most popular name among those who actually have the disease is "person (or people) with AIDS," or "PWA."

These distinctions are often important in many everyday situations. You might not have a problem recognizing a person in the advanced stages of AIDS. However, you would have no way of recognizing someone who is only HIV+. Yet, both people are equally infectious in terms of their ability to transmit HIV.

That fact troubles some health care workers, as you will see in Part II of the book. A doctor or nurse can recognize someone with full-blown AIDS and can take necessary precautions against infection. But the health care worker cannot recognize someone who is HIV+. Yet the health risks of certain contacts with the HIV+ person are as great as those with the person with full-blown AIDS. How does the health care worker protect herself or himself against the health risks of the HIV+ person?

Drug Treatment for AIDS

One of the great success stories of the AIDS epidemic is the wide variety of drugs that have been developed to use in treating the disease. Some of these drugs attack HIV itself. Others are used against AIDS-related diseases.

The first drug approved by the Food and Drug Administration (FDA) for use against HIV is called retrovir or azidothymidine (AZT). It works by preventing HIV from reproducing inside cells. It has been effective in slowing down the progress of AIDS, but it cannot completely stop the disease.

A second drug, chemically similar to AZT, was approved for use in October 1991. That drug is called dideoxyinosine, or ddI. A third antiviral drug, dideoxycytidine, or ddC, has also shown promise in the treatment of HIV infections but not been approved yet.

A number of other drugs are working their way through the stages of development and testing. Some of these drugs have been approved by the FDA for experimental or compassionate use. These terms mean that the drugs have not been formally approved by the FDA, but the agency has allowed drug manufacturers to distribute the drugs to people who cannot tolerate AZT or ddI or who meet other criteria. The FDA policy represents a dramatic change from previous policies about drug approval. This change has raised some issues among health professionals and the general public. Some of those issues will be discussed in Part II.

In addition to antiviral drugs like AZT and ddI, a great many other drugs are available for treating specific AIDS-related medical conditions. Also, literally hundreds of other anti-AIDS drugs have been and are being tested. Some of those drugs are being studied by scientists in laboratories around the world. Others are being tried out unofficially (and often illegally) both by scientists and by nonscientists. Some of the issues involved in drug testing are discussed in Part II.

No vaccine for AIDS is yet available. Finding a way to protect the body against HIV infection has turned out to be very difficult. HIV appears to be changing all the time. It has been difficult to find a vaccine that will protect against this constantly evolving virus.

A great deal of work is still going on, however, on the development of a vaccine. Human trials on one of these vaccine was begun in February of 1991.

Testing for AIDS

A test for HIV was first licensed for use in 1985. The test does not detect the virus itself but antibodies to the virus. Antibodies are chemicals produced by the body's immune system in order to fight against bacteria, viruses, and other materials that are foreign to the body. The test is called an ELISA test.[13] The term stands for enzyme-linked immunosorbant assay. As with any test, an ELISA test may produce both false positive and false negative results.

A false positive is a test that says a person does have an HIV infection when he or she really does not. A false negative is one that says the person does not have an HIV infection when, in fact, he or she really does.

The ELISA test produces a false positive about once in every one hundred to one thousand tests. Its rate of false negatives is very low.

A person who receives a positive result on an ELISA test usually is given a second, more accurate test, the Western blot test. The Western blot test has fewer false positives than does the ELISA test. Anyone who gets a positive result on both an ELISA and a Western blot test is considered to have an HIV infection.

Any HIV test also has another limitation. It takes a while for antibodies to begin to form after a person has been infected with HIV. That is, suppose that HIV enters your bloodstream today. An HIV test conducted tomorrow will not detect HIV antibodies. They have not had time to form in a measurable amount. In fact, it may be weeks or months before antibodies can be detected. During this time, blood tests will be negative even though infection has already occurred.

The problems of false positives, false negatives, and time lag in getting positive test results raise many questions about the use of HIV testing. Some of these questions are outlined in Part II.

Facts and Myths about HIV Transmission

A great deal of research has been done on the ways in which HIV can be transmitted. As you can imagine, people are very concerned about the possibility of contracting HIV from someone. Being infected with HIV is not like catching a cold. At the present time, an HIV infection results in very serious health problems that may result in death.

Medical researchers have found that HIV is actually a rather fragile virus. It does not survive outside of the human body very well. That means that the virus does not survive in the air, on plates or cups, on the skin, on door knobs or toilet seats, or in drinking water. Therefore, HIV cannot be transmitted by casual contacts such as shaking hands, touching, hugging, or simply being in the same room with an infected person.

This point has been an exceedingly important one in educating the general public about HIV infection. For a number of years, people were concerned that they might catch AIDS just by being around people who are HIV+. Many nonscientists have warned about the dangers of casual contact with those who are HIV+. For example, evangelist Pat Robertson was once quoted as saying that "anyone is in danger of catching AIDS if they are sneezed on, spit on, or even in the same room with people who carry the virus."[14]

The one place that HIV does survive is in body fluids such as blood, semen, vaginal secretions, and, in rare cases, breast milk. That fact means that almost the only way HIV can be transmitted from one person to another is through the exchange of body fluids.

Injecting drug users get AIDS because they share needles and other drug-use equipment. Suppose an infected drug user uses a needle to inject something into his or her blood stream. Some of that person's blood will remain in the needle. Now suppose a second drug user uses the same needle to inject a drug. The second person will receive not only the drug but also some of the first (infected) person's blood.

Blood, semen, and vaginal secretions may also be transferred during some kinds of sexual activities. If one of the persons involved in that activity is already infected, then HIV may be transferred along with the blood or semen.

The danger of HIV infection from blood transfusions has now been greatly reduced. All blood that is donated is now tested for HIV. If the virus is found, the blood is discarded. The risk of HIV infection from blood transfusions in 1991 was estimated at 1 in 40,000 to 153,000 units of transfused blood.[15]

These are the basic scientific facts about HIV infection and AIDS. As you read about AIDS-related issues, you may want to refer back to this chapter. People have every right to differ about their beliefs about these issues. However, whenever possible, those who disagree with each other should at least base their positions on accurate information.

4

AIDS:
An International Problem

AIDS is not a problem just for the United States. By 1990, the HIV epidemic had spread to 156 countries around the world. Figure 6 shows the number of AIDS cases reported as of June 1, 1990. Even the remote island of Greenland reported its first AIDS case as early as 1985.

The numbers in Figure 5 are probably somewhat misleading. More-developed countries, like the United States, Canada, Japan, and those in Western Europe, generally keep reliable, accurate health statistics. Less-developed countries, like those in Africa and South and Central America, have relatively poor record-keeping systems.

Many authorities believe that the number of AIDS cases in the less-developed countries is grossly underreported. The official count of AIDS cases is about 300,000 worldwide, but officials at the World Health Organization estimate that nearly three times that number actually exist. They also estimate that there are now at least ten million HIV+ people worldwide and predict that this number will jump to fifteen million to twenty million by the year 2000.[1]

Country	AIDS Cases	Country	AIDS Cases
United States	132,436	Canada	3,735
Uganda	12,444	Ivory Coast	3,647
Zaire	11,733	United Kingdom	3,137
Brazil	10,510	Haiti	2,331
France	9,718	Australia	1,824
Malawi	7,160	Trinidad & Tobago	557
Italy	6,068	Bahamas	437
Spain	5,295	Japan	189
West Germany	4,749	China	3
Mexico	4,268		

Fig. 5: AIDS Cases Worldwide (in selected nations, as of June 1, 1990)

HIV Infection in More-Developed Countries

In most of the more-developed countries of the world, patterns of HIV infection are similar to those in the United States. In France, England, and Germany, for example, the majority of HIV+ individuals are gay and bisexual men and IV drug users. In Spain, Greece, Italy, Ireland, and Scotland, IV drug users make up the majority of HIV+ cases.[2]

In other nations of the world, as in the United States, HIV infections have created difficult social and ethical issues. In Spain, for example, the government has initiated an aggressive campaign to promote condom use. Included in that campaign are television and billboard ads aimed at teenagers. Some ads picture a condom with the slogan, "Put it on yourself. Put it on him." In addition, Spain's Ministry of Health has begun handing out 1.5 million free condoms to teenagers.[3]

This campaign has stirred controversy in heavily Catholic Spain. Bishops of the Roman Catholic church are convinced that the ads will "excite and incite" teenagers into promiscuity. The end result, they warn, will be more unwanted pregnancies, abortions, and HIV infections.

The government says that the church is out of touch with the Spanish people. Spaniards may not like condom advertising, they say, but polls have shown that a large majority agree that the campaign is essential to stop the spread of HIV.

AIDS in the Third World

Probably the greatest concern for many world health authorities is the status of AIDS in Third World countries. In the nations of Africa, Asia, and South and Central America, the epidemic appears to be spreading like wildfire. The HIV epidemic is different in one important way in these countries from in the more-developed countries. In these countries, HIV is most often spread by heterosexual intercourse.

The statistics for Africa are truly terrifying. In some parts of central Africa—Malawi, Rwanda, Uganda, and Zambia—the rate of infection has reached 20 percent or more.[4] As many as nine out of ten female prostitutes in Nairobi are now HIV+. In 1985-86, 18 percent of the men visiting sexually transmitted disease (STD) clinics in that city were HIV+.[5] AIDS is now the leading cause of death among young men in some urban areas in Central Africa.

During the early years of the epidemic, most African nations denied the existence of AIDS in their countries. They claimed that Western reports of the disease were a "racist plot."[6]

A turning point in this attitude came when President Kenneth Kaunda of Zambia announced the death of his own son from AIDS. Slowly, African nations have come to realize and accept the enormity of their own HIV problems. They have begun to change their policies on the epidemic.

An example of this change is Uganda. There, President Yoweri Museveni had long opposed government programs for teaching about condom use. He thought such programs would only promote promiscuity.

In early 1991 he changed his mind. Advisors showed him projections that the nation's population would grow from its current level of sixteen million to twenty million by the year 2015 if nothing were done about the epidemic. Earlier estimates—assuming no AIDS epidemic—had been for a population of thirty-two million in 2015. The difference of twelve million represented those who could be expected to die of the epidemic in the next generation. President Museveni, confronted with this information, immediately changed his mind about condoms.[7]

AIDS in the Americas

Patterns of HIV infection in South and Central America and the Caribbean are similar to those in Africa. In 1991 the Pan American Health Organization estimated that more than three million people in the Western Hemisphere will be HIV+ by the mid-1990s. The organization estimated that 150,000 women in Latin American and the Caribbean are already infected. In Haiti, studies show that one in ten of all pregnant women is HIV+.[8]

Individual nations face somewhat different AIDS problems. In El Salvador, for example, HIV is spreading rapidly among female prostitutes. The government provides little or no education about the epidemic, and the women are unable to find alternative jobs that pay as well as prostitution. One physician in San Salvador warns that "AIDS here is increasing at a terrible rate and people aren't changing attitudes and customs."[9]

In Mexico City, AIDS is a special problem among hundreds of thousands of homeless children. Many young boys survive on the streets as prostitutes for older men. When the boys become infected with HIV, they then pass on the virus to their young friends through homosexual activity.

Most boys know about condoms. But they don't use them because they are regarded as "unmanly." "Most kids don't think there is any point in using one," a 12-year-old boy has said. "When your time is up, you die. We aren't afraid to die."[10]

Cuba has taken perhaps the most aggressive approach to the AIDS epidemic of any country in the world. Its policy is to test all Cubans for HIV. As of mid-1990, eight million of the nation's ten million residents had already been tested.

Those who test positive for the virus are quarantined for life in a fenced-in community. They are allowed to have family visits and are paid to work within the community. But they may never leave.

So far, 458 HIV+ people have been identified in the Cuban program. Of the 423 who are still alive, 70 percent are under the age of thirty-five. For whatever number of years these people have left to live, it will be spent within the fenced-in AIDS community.[11]

Perhaps the most serious HIV problem in Latin America can be found in Brazil. Over the past three years, the number of new HIV cases has been doubling every six months. The city of Sao Paulo alone may have 100,000 AIDS cases by the year 2000.

Part of the problem in Brazil appears to be people's attitudes about sexuality. Education programs are not very successful because Brazilians are embarrassed to talk about sexual topics. On the other hand, they tend to be very liberal about sexual behaviors. Bisexuality, in particular, is generally accepted and widely practiced. Married men think nothing of having sex with another man. "It's just one of those things he does with no moral consequence," according to a Brazilian scientist.[12]

As a result, Brazilian women are at serious risk for HIV infection. That fact, in turn, presents the additional possibility that HIV infections among newborn children will also increase.

Women and AIDS

Health authorities are especially concerned about the growing number of women who are contracting HIV infections worldwide. The World Health Organization (WHO) has estimated that some three million women world-wide are infected with the virus. About one-third of the 1.3 million cases of AIDS so far have been women.[13]

As of 1990, three in five cases of HIV infection worldwide resulted from heterosexual intercourse. By the year 2000, that fraction is expected to rise to 75-80 percent. That change means that an even larger fraction of women will become HIV+.

The effects on women will be especially severe in certain locations. For example, 52 percent of the adult AIDS cases in Uganda are women. Also, WHO predicts that most of the two million who will die of AIDS in the 1990s will come from the sub-Sahara regions of Africa.[14]

As in the United States, the tragedy for women will extend to their children. WHO has estimated that 30 percent of the children born to HIV+ women will also become infected. The final result may be that as many as ten million HIV+ children will be born during the 1990s.

Many people in the United States are beginning to have some hope that the HIV epidemic may be coming under control . . . at least in some locations and with some groups of individuals. That trend is anything but the case in many other parts of the world. African and Latin American nations are just beginning to see the size of the AIDS problems awaiting them in the next generation. At the moment, it looks as though the situation in these nations will become much worse before it becomes any better.

II
THE ISSUES

5

Testing for HIV Infection

AIDS is an infectious disease that has serious consequences for both society and the individual. One might think that HIV testing would be a popular concept. It would often be to the advantage to both society and individuals to know who is HIV+.

This is especially true because of some special characteristics of an HIV infection. A person may remain asymptomatic (show no signs of infection) for a long time after infection. In many cases, people have not developed AIDS-related symptoms until ten years or more after being infected with HIV.

There are probably hundreds of thousands or millions of asymptomatic HIV+ men and women in the United States and Canada today. You can not tell from their appearance that they have been infected with HIV. They often look, act, and feel completely healthy.

But these healthy-looking, healthy-feeling people are infectious. They can transmit HIV to a healthy person through some kinds of sexual contact, by donating blood, or by sharing needles.

HIV testing would seem to be especially valuable in identifying these asymptomatic individuals. Health workers could use the information to help limit the spread of the disease, and infected individuals could start getting treatment for the infection.

But the practice of HIV antibody testing is surrounded by a great deal of controversy. Many people who are at risk for HIV infection flatly refuse to be tested. Other people—including those who are at risk and those who are not—believe that testing should be done only under very strict conditions. Then, the results of those tests should be carefully controlled and used for only limited purposes.

Should People Be Afraid to Get Tested Because They Might Prove HIV+?

Given the widespread acceptance of testing for tuberculosis and other contagious diseases, how can we explain the concerns that so many people have about HIV testing? These concerns are often based on the fact that being identified as HIV+ can create serious problems for a person.

In most diseases (although certainly not all), those who are ill are viewed with concern and compassion. Public health authorities, government officials, and the general public really want to help people who are sick. They are willing to do what they can to treat patients and help them feel better.

That often is not the case with AIDS patients. Instead of care and compassion, the attitude is often "Who cares?" or "I'm glad they're sick."

One writer has suggested that the AIDS epidemic really involves two diseases.[1] One is the medical condition resulting from HIV infection. The second "disease" is the fear that HIV negative people have of the AIDS virus. The writer calls this second condition Acute Fear Regarding AIDS, or AFRAIDS. People with AIDS and those who are HIV+ have to deal not only with being ill but also with the way other people react to that fact.

The existence of AFRAIDS means that HIV testing involves much more than health matters. Imagine that you are someone who is at risk for HIV infection. You really would like to be tested for HIV. You know that a negative test result will set your mind at ease. Even a positive result will allow you to start medical treatment that will help fight the disease.

But you know very well how many people feel about individuals who get AIDS. What will happen if your boss, your landlord, your insurance company, or someone else gets information about your test results? Will they want to fire you, throw you out of your apartment, cancel your health and life insurance?

Those fears are not imaginary. There have been any number of cases where something like this has happened. For example:

- Paramedics and sheriff's deputies in Birmingham, Alabama, kept lists of local residents known or believed to have AIDS.[2]

- Police in Montgomery, Alabama, compiled a list of residents who were suspected of being HIV+.[3]

- An employee at the Veteran's Administration Hospital in St. Petersburg, Florida, released the names of AIDS patients to a person outside the hospital.[4]

- In Sacramento, California, three computers containing the names of people with AIDS were stolen from the state's Department of Health offices.[5]

- A Job Corps worker in Dayton, Ohio, was dropped from the program when found to be HIV+. The director of the program said the worker was a health risk to coworkers.[6]

- An elementary school teacher in Nova Scotia was removed from his job when he tested positive for HIV.[7]

- A mail carrier in White Plains, New York, refused to deliver mail to an AIDS task force office because he was afraid of catching HIV.[8]

- A student at Howard University in Washington, D.C., was refused treatment for an attempted suicide when doctors learned she was HIV+. Instead, they left her strapped in a bed, "wallowing in her own feces" for five days.[9]

- Two lesbians working at Johns Hopkins University were fired because coworkers feared they would catch HIV from them.[10]

- Delta Airlines announced—and later rescinded—a policy to exclude people with AIDS from all its flights.[11]

- People refused to serve on a jury for a trial in which the defendant had AIDS.[12]

- A municipal swimming pool in Williamson, West Virginia, was shut down after a man with AIDS swam in it.[13]

Situations like these are not uncommon.[14] They tend to make a person at risk for HIV infection have second thoughts about the wisdom of being tested.

Drs. Robert Blendon and Karen Donelan have studied the everyday problems facing people with AIDS or people who are HIV+. They have concluded that there are certain realities such people have to understand. Among those realities are the following:

- Reality 1: Americans with AIDS will likely face discrimination from a substantial segment of the population.

- Reality 2: People with AIDS may face loss of personal privacy and, possibly, restrictions on their civil rights.

- Reality 3: People with AIDS may confront a significant minority of Americans who show signs of intolerance and outright hostility toward them.

- Reality 4: Patients with AIDS face a significant risk of losing their jobs and, consequently, their health insurance.

- Reality 5: People with AIDS face the risk of losing their housing or not having accommodations available when they require new living arrangements.[15]

Should People Testing Positive for HIV Be Afraid of Other People's Attitudes Toward AIDS?

So the doubts that many people have about HIV testing are not based on the tests themselves but on the way those tests might be used. Anyone who tests positive for HIV has a right to wonder how friends, neighbors, employers, the government, and others might use that information.

What is there about HIV infection and AIDS that makes this disease so different from other infectious diseases? At least two factors make the AIDS epidemic unusual.

First, simply as a medical problem, AIDS appears to be an especially terrifying disease to many people. The disease is relatively new, it cannot be cured, and—rightly or wrongly—people still have many questions about the ways it can be transmitted and the probable end result of an HIV infection.

Ryan White's story illustrates how badly people can behave to an otherwise normal person because of their fears of AIDS. We can understand how a person at risk for HIV infection might be frightened by the prospect of other people learning about his or her HIV status and, for that reason, refusing to be tested.

Second, a large majority of people who have been infected with HIV are gay, bisexual males, injecting drug users, or their sexual partners. Society often regards men and women in these groups as sick, sinful, criminal, or, at the very least, undesirable. Their lives are often thought to have less value than those of heterosexual, nondrug users.

This attitude is reflected in the statements of some public officials. For many years, these officials were simply not concerned about the AIDS epidemic as long as it affected only "those people," meaning gay and bisexual men and injecting drug users. Sen. Jesse Helms expressed this viewpoint in a comment he made on the floor of the U.S. Senate in 1987. "I guess you can say as long as this disease is confined among homosexuals, no real danger. It is bad, but they should realize this . . . But now, when we are dealing with the other side of this coin, where children can catch it, . . . [there is a serious problem we must address]."

In fact, a few individuals thought that AIDS was a good thing since it helped rid society of some of its worst elements. The gay magazine *The Advocate* frequently carries reports of individuals or groups who praise AIDS as a solution to society's problems with homosexuality.[16]

A number of writers have commented on the slow response of the United States government to the AIDS epidemic.[17] The disease was first identified during the early years of the Reagan administration. The 1980s were a decade of conservatism, both in government and in the nation at large. Many government officials thought that gay and bisexual males and injecting drug users were simply "getting what they deserved."

For example, Patrick Buchanan, presidential hopeful in the 1992 elections, conservative columnist, television panelist, and former advisor to President Ronald Reagan, wrote that AIDS was a sign of "the wrath of God." Gay men "have declared war on nature," he said, "and now nature is exacting an awful retribution."[18]

This viewpoint is one that has been held by a number of religious leaders, some medical writers, and many members of the general public. The Reverend Jerry Falwell is reported to have said that "AIDS is the wrath of God upon homosexuals." And the Anglican dean of Sydney, Australia, apparently announced that "gays have blood on their hands."[19]

A survey of evangelical Christians found strong support for this opinion. Thirty-seven percent of those interviewed by the magazine *Christianity Today* agreed with the statement that "AIDS is a judgment from God on homosexuals and drug users."[20]

An example of President Reagan's attitude toward AIDS was expressed on October 28, 1988. On that date, the president signed a bill declaring the *preceding* month as AIDS Awareness Month.

Although members of the president's administration apparently joked about the disease in private,[21] Reagan himself never mentioned the word "AIDS" in public until September 17, 1985, four years after the epidemic had begun. On that date, he explained that he understood why parents would not want their children "in school with these kids" who have "AIDS."[22]

Critics have often pointed out how differently the government and the general public responded to the AIDS crisis compared to "Legionnaire's disease" in 1976 or the "Tylenol scare" of 1982.[23] In the latter cases, the response by public health officials was quick and efficient. In each case, only a handful of people died, compared to the tens of thousands who have died from AIDS. The difference was that Legionnaire's disease and the Tylenol deaths affected "good, normal people," not "perverts and druggies."[24]

As a result of these social attitudes, many people who are at risk for HIV infection have doubts about being tested. They realize that AIDS is not just another medical condition. People who compare AIDS to other infectious diseases are not thinking about the social, economic, political, and psychological aspects of the disease. They may believe that public health officials should treat people with AIDS and those who are HIV+ just as they would people who have tuberculosis, malaria, or some other infectious disease.

But that notion is naive. People with tuberculosis, malaria, and other infectious diseases are normally not hated, feared, and despised by the general public. The goal of a testing program for these diseases is probably totally compassionate, aimed at helping sick people. A person who is at risk for HIV may be unlikely to believe that HIV testing programs have such completely compassionate objectives.

Should Test Results Be Kept Confidential? Should Testing Be Voluntary or Mandatory?

The controversy over HIV testing creates a difficult dilemma. On the one hand, HIV testing can be very useful. Test results can be helpful to public health authorities, to people in high risk groups, and perhaps to others. On the other hand, some methods must be found to protect a person against the improper use of test results.

Many experts now think that two guidelines are necessary in any HIV testing program. Those guidelines are as follows:

1. The test results must be kept confidential.

2. The test must be voluntary.

The principle of confidentiality means that test results are made known only to the person who is tested and to anyone else he or she designates. A person who tests positive for HIV infection, for example, might want his doctor and his rabbi to see his test results but no one else.

Confidentiality is a common principle in medicine. When you go to a doctor, you do not expect the doctor to discuss your case with anyone who doesn't need to know about it. So why should people who are at risk for HIV infection worry about confidentiality?

One reason is that many of these individuals simply don't trust doctors, nurses, government officials, medical authorities, or others who might see their test records. They know that people in those groups are not all that different from the general public. They, as much as anyone else in society, may hate and/or fear people who are at risk for HIV infection.

Studies consistently show that health care workers often hold very negative views toward people with AIDS. In one case, 30 percent of a sample of physicians and nurses interviewed reported that they felt more negatively about homosexuals since the emergence of AIDS. Twelve percent of those health care workers agreed that people with AIDS were "getting what they deserved."[25] People at risk for HIV infection may be justified in their concerns about confidentiality of some medical workers.

Violations of confidentiality are not unusual in other fields also. For example, there have been many reports of such instances in the U.S. military, where testing for HIV infection is now mandatory. Imagine that you are taking a required HIV test to join the army. The results of that test will probably be entered into a computer with those of thousands of other recruits. How many people will be able to look at those results? One research team discusses a number of instances in which members of the military who tested positive for HIV infection were reported to base commanders by company doctors. Those individuals were then discharged because of their HIV status or because they had admitted to high risk behavior, such as homosexual acts.[26]

One way to ensure confidentiality is by making tests anonymous. A person who goes to a clinic for an HIV test is usually given an identifying number. When the person calls in for the test results, he or she only has to tell the clinic his or her number. In many cases, no one at the clinic or the laboratory knows who has that number. So the test is completely anonymous.

This system reduces the number of people who know a person's test results (often to zero). It increases the chances of confidentiality. However, in some clinics, at least one worker may know those results. So a person may still be concerned about how private his or her results will really be.

Is Medical Information Private? Does Society Have the Right to Protect Itself by Having Test Results Known?

Confidentiality has another side. Suppose a cafeteria worker with tuberculosis visits her doctor. And imagine that the worker asks the doctor to keep her illness a secret. Should the doctor do so?

Probably not. Tuberculosis is a highly contagious disease. The worker is likely to transmit her infection to others at the cafeteria. The doctor probably should insist that the worker give up her job.

This example reminds us that the issue of confidentiality can involve two rights:

1. The right of a person to keep medical information private.
2. The right of society to protect itself against communicable diseases.

A person who has tuberculosis is different from someone who is HIV+. Tuberculosis spreads easily, by casual contact. HIV does not. HIV is most commonly spread only by certain types of sexual acts and by sharing of needles.

A doctor might insist that someone with tuberculosis give up a cafeteria job. But that would probably not be necessary with a person who is HIV+.

In Which Circumstances Should Testing Be Voluntary or Mandatory?

People who debate issues of HIV testing tend to agree about the issue of confidentiality. Those same people may hold very different views on another testing issue: voluntary vs. mandatory testing.

Voluntary testing means that a person has a choice about taking the test or not. Under mandatory testing, certain groups of people or individuals are required to take the test, whether they want to or not.

The concept of mandatory testing for HIV involves a number of practical problems. For example, who should be covered by a mandatory testing program—All Americans? All single men over the age of 21? All gay men? All IV drug users?

You can see the difficulties presented by the concept of mandatory testing. Could we possibly afford to test all Americans or all single men over the age of 21? How could we identify all gay men? Could we really arrange to test all injecting drug users?

Partly because of these practical questions, those who favor mandatory testing usually focus on specific groups. For example, many agencies of the federal government now require mandatory HIV testing of all employees. Such tests are now required by such agencies as the Department of Defense, the Peace Corps, the Job Corps, and the State Department. Some states also require that prostitutes and/or prisoners be tested.

Agencies that require HIV testing have offered a number of reasons for this policy. For example, some of the justifications offered by federal agencies include the need to protect workers from reactions to vaccinations, to prevent the spread of HIV through direct blood transfusions, to protect workers from diseases that are common in parts of the world other than the United States, and to avoid the hiring of employees who will eventually become a drain on the agency's medical programs.

Critics of mandatory testing have countered each of these arguments. For example, these critics state there has been only a single case of an HIV-infected person having had a reaction to a vaccination. Also, the availability of artificial blood makes the need for direct blood transfusions very small. In addition, people who are HIV+ do not appear to be at risk for any of the major diseases with which they might come into contact elsewhere in the world. Finally, the long incubation period for AIDS suggests that government agencies are probably not the ones who will have to deal with the ultimate cost of the disease.[27]

One possible method for implementing mandatory testing has been called the "turnstile" approach. This concept was first proposed by William F. Buckley in 1986.[28] Buckley pointed out that people pass through certain "turnstiles" at various points in their lives. For example, they may enter high school, go on to college, marry, join the armed forces, apply for jobs, and so on. One form of mandatory testing would be to test people at each of these "turnstiles." For example, anyone who applies for college might be required to have an HIV test. The test might also be part of the marriage license application procedure.

The one organization to have adopted the concept of mandatory "turnstile" testing most widely is the United States government. During his term of office, President Ronald Reagan recommended a massive program of mandatory HIV testing. The mandatory testing programs described above are the result of Reagan's recommendations.

Some critics ask what the value of "turnstile" tests like these are. In theory, the tests could be used to help counsel and advise people who are HIV+. But no mandatory program has that as an objective. Instead, the aim of these programs is to eliminate anyone who tests positive. The person is excluded from the military, the Peace Corps, the State Department, or some other government job.

But does that help reduce the spread of HIV? Will a person be less likely to transmit HIV if he or she works for IBM rather than the State Department?

In fact, mandatory programs may have results opposite those intended. A person may avoid applying for a job where HIV testing is required. He or she may be concerned about the use to which the test results are put. California's former director of public health, Dr. Kenneth Kizer, presented the argument this way. "I believe that individuals who engage in high-risk behavior," he said, "have a responsibility to voluntarily undergo a test to determine if they are carrying the AIDS virus. Across-the-board [mandatory] testing, however, sends the wrong message and would be a great waste of limited funds."[29]

A voluntary program might be less frightening and less threatening than a mandatory program. The person might gain some valuable information—his or her HIV status—from the voluntary program.

Another problem with mandatory testing is that it must be repeated on a regular basis. A person who receives a negative result on one test may become infected shortly after the test. Any program that really wants to keep track of those who are HIV+ will have to continue testing people over and over again.

Continued testing means that mandatory programs are often very expensive. Some critics ask whether the small number of positive results produced by such programs are really worth their expense.[30]

Finally, many people object to mandatory testing because it presents a serious threat to confidentiality. Any one who worries about the loss of confidentiality for voluntary testing will probably be even more concerned about the effects of mandatory programs.

One authority has suggested that one has to assess each specific recommendation for mandatory testing. The criterion must be, he says, "whether the policy offers benefits sufficient to outweigh the intrusions into liberty and informational privacy." In his judgment, this standard is seldom met, which accounts for the fact that "public health officials have consistently favored AIDS education as the best strategy for prevention and opposed most mandatory testing."[31]

Should People Who Practice High Risk Behaviors Volunteer to Be Tested?

People who practice high risk behaviors have to make a difficult personal choice about HIV testing. At first glance, the decision appears to be an easy one. Whether one tests positive or negative, the information gained can be very helpful. On the one hand, a negative HIV test would certainly be good news. If nothing else, it can provide a sense of relief. Also, a negative test might encourage one to redouble efforts to avoid high risk behavior, such as avoiding injecting drugs and abstaining from sex or practicing only safe sex.

On the other hand, a positive test result would suggest that one should begin to think about medical treatment as soon as possible. Studies have shown that people who take AZT before AIDS symptoms appear live longer than those who do not. Thus, a person who knows that he or she is HIV+ may be able to start taking AZT or ddI immediately. This treatment may slow down the progress of the infection.

But many people are not convinced that HIV testing is a good idea for them. They may be frightened by the kind of future that an HIV+ diagnosis suggests. Even when they recognize the encouraging progress that medical science has made, they may not want to take the chance of learning they are HIV+. Again, right or wrong, worry and fear may be more important factors than accurate knowledge about one's HIV status.

These concerns have special significance for some people who engage in high risk behaviors. For example, people who are recovering from drug addiction may not have the psychological strength to deal with a positive HIV test result. Such individuals might be better off waiting before taking an HIV test.[32]

Also, practical factors might affect a person's decision about taking an HIV test. Many people cannot afford adequate medical care. What would they do if they tested positive? They might well not be able to begin the medical treatments they would need.

6

Using Test Results

HIV testing raises many questions. The person who is tested will probably want to know his or her HIV status. But does that person's doctor, employer, or landlord need to know? Should the information be given to the local public health department or some other agency of the government? Some of the most difficult issues surrounding the AIDS epidemic concern the way in which HIV test results are used.

Probably the first and most obvious use of HIV test results is for the individual. A person who tests positive for HIV knows that he or she has contracted an infectious disease that requires medical attention.

Test results may also have value for the society at large. One way to limit the spread of any infectious disease is to identify those individuals who carry the disease. That is a major task of the public health profession.

Exactly how can society, particularly—public health workers or other private or government agencies—use HIV test results in an ethical way?

What can people legitimately do with test results that will help protect people in the community from AIDS without violating the rights of those who are HIV+?

These questions lie at the heart of many AIDS-related issues facing the world today.

A number of possible uses have been suggested for HIV test results. Some of these proposals involve familiar public health practices that may or may not also be applicable to the AIDS epidemic. For example, some people would like to have access to HIV test results in order to trace the sex and drug partners of those who test positive for HIV. Other proposals for the use of HIV test results have little or nothing to do with public (or private) health issues. For example, some insurance companies would like to use HIV test results to decide whether a person qualifies for insurance coverage or not.

Should Positive HIV Tests Be Reported to Health Officials?

Maintaining public health by preventing the spread of disease has long been regarded as a legitimate responsibility of the individual states in this country. Public health laws regarding the testing for and reporting of infectious disease go back to the eighteenth century.[1] Today, for example, the name of anyone who tests positive for syphilis, gonorrhea, or any other sexually transmitted disease must be reported to the state health department and to the national Centers for Disease Control (CDC).

Some people have argued that AIDS and HIV infection should also be defined as "reportable diseases." That is, like anyone who is infected with syphilis and gonorrhea, a person with AIDS or a person who is HIV+ should also be reported to state and federal health agencies. Such a practice, they say, is only a matter of good public health practice. Mandatory reporting laws can be a valuable tool in helping reduce the spread of the disease. If states and the federal government require mandatory reporting of relatively mild diseases such as gonorrhea, they certainly should mandate the reporting of HIV infection and AIDS, it is argued.

In fact, mandatory reporting of AIDS is required by all states and the federal government. However, the same is not true for HIV infections. As of late 1991, only eight states—Alaska, Alabama, Idaho, Minnesota, North Dakota, South Dakota, South Carolina, and Virginia—required that the names of all HIV+ people be reported to state public health agencies. An additional seventeen states had a "mixed" law, requiring the reporting of HIV infections under some circumstances but not under others.[2]

This difference may be difficult to understand. People who are HIV+ are as infectious as those who have AIDS.

If Mandatory Reporting of AIDS Is a Good Public Health Practice, Isn't the Mandatory Reporting of a Positive HIV Test also a Good Idea?

One answer is that the purpose of reporting test results is to help stop the spread of a disease. But studies have shown that people who know that their test results will be reported to a government agency are less likely to get tested.[3] If those people are not tested, then a major tool in disease control is lost.

Most states with large populations appear to accept that line of reasoning so far. California, New York, New Jersey, Florida, and other states with large numbers of HIV+ individuals still do not require the reporting of HIV test results to state agencies.

Still, it is not clear how long states and the federal government will continue to treat HIV infections differently from other contagious diseases. Dr. Ronald Bayer, associate professor of public health at Columbia University, has called this special treatment of HIV infections as "exceptionalism." In Bayer's view, governments will eventually recognize the HIV infections must be treated like other communicable diseases. "Inevitably," he has written, "HIV exceptionalism will be viewed as a relic of the epidemic's first years."[4]

Should People with Positive Test Results Be Quarantined?

"Every member of the [American] population should be blood tested every month to detect the presence of antibodies against [AIDS], and all those found to be infected should be isolated compulsorily, immediately, and permanently."[5]

This proposal was made in 1987 by Christopher Monckton, former special advisor to Great Britain's Primer Minister Margaret Thatcher. His suggestion is typical of some of the most extreme proposals for using HIV test results. If everyone who is HIV+ can be identified and quarantined (isolated from other people), the argument goes, the epidemic can be brought under control.

Other public figures have endorsed this concept. In a 1987 interview, Sen. Jesse Helms of North Carolina said, "I may be the most radical person you've talked to about AIDS, but I think that somewhere along the line that we are going to have to quarantine, if we are really going to contain this disease."[6]

Other government officials have also considered some form of quarantine for people who are HIV+. James Mason, former head of the CDC, admitted that various plans for quarantining people who are HIV+ had been discussed.[7]

Any plan to identify and quarantine all HIV+ individuals would involve enormous practical problems. If for no other reason, the cost of testing 250,000,000 Americans on a regular basis would appear to doom any such plan. Still, modifications of the quarantine proposal on a more limited basis are sometimes popular.

Three states—Colorado, Idaho, and Kentucky—have passed laws that specifically allow people who have AIDS or who are HIV+ to be quarantined. Other states have adopted laws that permit public health officials to quarantine such individuals in specific situations. For example, laws in Alabama, Connecticut, Indiana, Minnesota, and North Carolina allow public health officials to quarantine people with communicable diseases who are endangering the public health.[8]

Some examples in which quarantining has been used are the following:

- A prostitute in Florida who was HIV+ was ordered to stay at home. She had to wear a special signaling device that notified police if she traveled more than 200 feet from her telephone.[9]

- A 14-year-old boy infected with HIV was confined by a judge to a local psychiatric hospital. The judge believed the boy was too active sexually and therefore was likely to spread HIV to others.[10]

A form of quarantining is also practiced by many governmental agencies. For example, since 1985, the Department of Defense has required HIV testing of all civilian and military personnel. Anyone who tests positive is separated from the military or prevented from joining it. In this way, the Department of Defense quarantines HIV+ people from the military, although not from society at large.

Strong objections have been raised to the concept of quarantining people with AIDS and people who are HIV+. One historian and psychiatrist has listed two reasons to oppose the practice. First, previous attempts to control communicable disease by quarantine have been largely unsuccessful. Second, increased information about the nature of HIV infection will help calm the irrational fears that have led to calls for quarantines.[11]

People who object to quarantines also point out the serious issues of individual rights that are involved. The United States has a long history of respect for individual rights and freedoms. There must be a very serious threat to the general society if those rights and freedoms are to be curtailed. So far, the existence of AIDS and HIV infections do not pose that kind of threat, critics say.[12]

Other proposals have been made for identifying and "marking" people who are HIV+. One of the best known of these proposals was offered by columnist William F. Buckley in 1986. Buckley suggested that all HIV+ people be tattooed. The tattoo would be placed on the arm of an injecting drug user or the buttock of a gay or bisexual male. The tattoo would warn other people that the person was infected with HIV. An uninfected person could avoid sharing a needle or engaging in high risk sexual behavior with the tattooed person.[13]

Buckley's suggestion about tattooing drew some outraged letters in response to his idea. One writer described Buckley's idea as "an astonishingly nasty bit of demagoguery." Another called his idea "arrogant, insensitive, and sensational." He compared Buckley's suggestion to the tattooing that was used in Nazi Germany as a way of "keeping track of undesirables marked for destruction."[14]

Should Test Results Be Used to Contact Sex and Drug Partners of an HIV+ Person?

Information about HIV+ people can also be used to notify their drug and sex partners. Today, anyone who tests positive for syphilis, gonorrhea, or other sexually transmitted diseases is asked to name his or her partners. Those partners can then be contacted. They can be told that they have been in contact with someone who is infected with one of these diseases. This procedure is known as contact tracing.

The same procedure could be used for HIV+ people. In fact, some states now require that all persons infected with HIV give health officials the names of their partners. In addition, it has been estimated that at least 80 percent of all physicians support this practice.[15]

Notifying an infected person's contacts can be a valuable public health practice. Often those contacts may not realize they have been exposed to disease. They may already be infected without realizing it. They may also be passing the infection on to their other contacts.

Contact tracing can be an important tool in stopping the spread of an epidemic like AIDS. If people know they have been exposed to a disease, they may try to avoid spreading it to others.

Although contact tracing is an excellent idea from a public health standpoint, there are still objections to the procedure. For example, people may not want to have their drug and sex partners notified. Rightly or wrongly, they may be embarrassed or afraid to have their partners find out their HIV status. If they knew that they will be asked to name their partners, they may avoid being tested at all. In that case, contact tracing would actually defeat the purpose of HIV testing.

As an alternative to asking a person about his or her partners, medical workers may encourage the individual to do the necessary notifying himself or herself. The worker may also provide information and assistance needed in making these notifications.

The Presidential Commission on the Human Immunodeficiency Virus Epidemic in 1988 strongly supported the concept of contact tracing. The commission said that "[t]he public health department has an obligation to ensure that any partners are aware of their exposure to the virus." The commission also emphasized the importance of respecting the confidentiality of the person who was tested.[16]

Should Couples Be Tested for HIV When Applying for a Marriage License?

In a May 31, 1987, speech, President Ronald Reagan recommended that all couples be tested for HIV when applying for a marriage license. Surveys suggest that about 80 percent of the general public support this idea.[17] As of April 1987, thirty states were considering laws that would require HIV testing by marriage applicants.

This concept is certainly not new. For many years a blood test for syphilis has been required for a marriage license in all states. Certainly a man or woman has the right to know if his or her future mate is infected with a deadly disease.

The test makes sense for another reason. A person might not want to ask a future mate about possible HIV infection. Husband and wife are supposed to trust each other. Does asking about a person's previous drug and/or sexual experiences indicate real trust? A person who is uncomfortable in dealing with this issue might want to have a test that will answer that question more easily.

By 1988 two states—Illinois and Louisiana—had actually passed laws requiring HIV testing for a marriage license. But the laws did not necessarily work as legislators had expected. In Illinois, for example, thousands of couples crossed state lines to get marriage licenses. They went to Wisconsin, Indiana, or another nearby state to get married. In this way, they could avoid being tested for HIV.

Experts also point out the high cost of premarital HIV testing. So far, HIV infection among heterosexual men and women who are not IV drug users has been very low. We would not expect to find many HIV+ people applying for marriage license, they say. By one estimate, it would cost about $83,000 to find each HIV+ person who applies for a marriage license.[18] Authorities wonder if it would be worth that expense to require HIV testing

68

of all marriage license applicants. Louisiana and Illinois apparently agreed with this idea. By 1990, both states had repealed their HIV testing laws.

Should Insurance Companies Be Allowed to Test for HIV?

Most insurance companies are very much interested in knowing a person's HIV status. This interest has nothing to do with helping a person deal with his or her health problems or with trying to limit the spread of AIDS. It involves business decisions that have to be made about selling a product: insurance policies.

Suppose someone applying for a health insurance policy has been infected with HIV. That person will probably develop AIDS eventually. He or she will have a lot of very expensive medical bills.

The average annual cost for patients with AIDS in 1991 was $32,000, of which $24,000 was for hospital care and $8,000 for other medical services. The average lifetime cost for hospital care for an AIDS patient in 1991 was $83,500.[19] The total cost of the first 10,000 cases of AIDS was estimated to be more than $6.3 billion.[20]

You can see the problem this presents for insurance companies. A large fraction of the cost of AIDS is paid by private insurance companies. Any company with a large number of HIV+ policy holders is in trouble. It may not be able to pay all its claims and still stay in business.

In fact, some authorities fear that the cost of AIDS may "destroy the insurance business as we know it."[21] That is the prediction of Barbara Lautzenheiser, an insurance consultant in Connecticut. She thinks that companies will have to raise all premium rates, not just those for people with AIDS or those who are HIV+. Eventually, she fears, the premiums will get so high that ordinary people will no longer be able to afford insurance.

Other critics agree. One writer sees no reason that AIDS should get special treatment. He claims that "AIDS victims suffer tragically, but so do millions of cancer patients." He asks "Why should AIDS be unique, exempt from the logic of insurance?"[22]

Not everyone agrees that AIDS poses such a threat to the insurance business. A survey conducted by the Office of Technology Assessment in 1988 showed that, in actual fact, AIDS is probably no more expensive than many other serious diseases. The survey found that at least fifteen other insurable diseases were more expensive than was AIDS.[23]

Insurance companies already test for a number of conditions that are potentially very expensive. They can deny a policy to anyone with a number of diseases such as diabetes mellitus, leukemia, severe obesity, severe angina, epilepsy, cirrhosis of the liver, and lupus. They can issue restricted policies for many other conditions, including asthma, arthritis, gout, glaucoma, gallstones, peptic ulcer, and colitis.[24]

So you can see why an insurance company would also want to test an applicant for HIV. Many companies now include such a test in their general physical examination. A person who tests positive for HIV can be rejected for insurance.

So far, two states—California and Wisconsin—have made this practice illegal. Some other states are considering laws like those in California and Wisconsin. But in the great majority of states, an insurance company can still require an applicant to have an HIV test.[25]

Insurance companies also use other methods to screen out HIV+ applicants. For instance, they know that certain geographical areas are likely to contain many high risk individuals. The Castro neighborhood in San Francisco, for example, is widely known as the home of many gay men. An insurance company may decide to reject all applicants received from the Castro neighborhood. It may tell agents not to accept any application that has a Castro zip code on it.

This practice is known as "red-lining." Red-lining is illegal. Suppose you are a married woman living in the Castro neighborhood. Red-lining would prevent you from getting an insurance policy just because you have the "wrong" zip code. Although insurance companies know this practice is illegal, they have sometimes tried to use it in the AIDS epidemic.

Companies can use other methods to locate high risk individuals. They can ask question on their applications that identify such individuals. For example, a company might suspect that a 35-year old single male nurse might be gay.

That kind of stereotyping is foolish today. Most male nurses are not gay. In fact, most 35-year-old single men are not gay.

But a company might be willing to take the chance it had guessed correctly in this case. Practices of this kind are also illegal.

Finally, insurance companies have one last resort when faced with the cost of policyholders who have AIDS. They can simply cancel the policies. In 1990, for example, Great Republic Insurance Company canceled group health insurance policies covering 14,000 people in California. A number of people holding these policies were ill with cancer, AIDS, and other major illnesses.

Great Republic said they had made this decision because the policy was not profitable. Policyholders could change to a new policy, but the premiums for the new policy would be much higher than they were for the old one.[26] This method of dealing with the problem of insuring people with AIDS is apparently not uncommon.[27]

States have tried to find a balance that will solve this problem. They recognize that insurance companies have the right to make a profit. But they also realize that people who are HIV+ need health and life insurance. They have written laws that try to meet both needs at once.

Most insurance companies want to find a solution to this problem, too. In 1985 the National Association of Insurance Commissioners appointed a special task force on AIDS and insurance. That task force developed a set of recommendations for state legislation on this issue. Those recommendations included the prohibition of redlining or the consideration of sexual orientation in the determination of insurability.[28]

One solution has been a new type of policy developed in the state of California. The California Major Risk Medical Insurance Program helps insurance companies provide health coverage to people who would normally not qualify for insurance. People with AIDS and HIV+ people fall into this category. Insurance premiums are set at about 25 percent above premiums for a healthy person. The extra cost to an insurance company in paying a patient's bills is covered by the state. The money comes from a special tax on tobacco products passed by voters in 1989.[29]

Should a Woman Who Is HIV+ Be Allowed to Become Pregnant?

The increasing visibility of HIV+ women and women with AIDS has raised new questions about the advisability of HIV testing among women of child-bearing age. One question focuses on the possibility of an HIV+ woman becoming pregnant.

Already, thousands of children born to HIV+ men and women develop AIDS each year. In 1991, 800 babies contracted AIDS from their infected mothers, an increase of 100 percent in just three years. The President's Commission on the Human Immunodeficiency Virus Epidemic reported in 1988 that the problem presented by such babies was "one of the most heart-rending the Commission had encountered."[30]

Many authorities are concerned that the social and economic costs of caring for all these children could be staggering. An editorial in the *Journal of the American Medical Association* warned that HIV infection would soon become the largest single cause of infant mortality in the nation's inner cities.[31]

What can be done to prevent this? Some individuals would like to reduce the number of HIV+ babies by preventing women infected with HIV from becoming pregnant or from giving birth to a child. One pair of authors has warned that "societies may soon have to wrestle with many difficult questions, including . . . the suitability of infected individuals for marriage and natural parenthood."[32]

One letter-writer criticized this idea by pointing out that "[b]oth moral sensibilities and our constitutional tradition revolt at the notion that classes of adults—defined in terms of biologic factors—be barred from marriage." In rebuttal, the original authors pointed out that they did not personally approve of restricting motherhood. However, they believed such actions might be inevitable in the future. "We can predict," they wrote, "that as the pandemic widens and deepens in our society, increasingly powerful voices will be heard calling for such state-imposed restrictions."[33]

The notion of limiting a woman's right to bear children is not entirely new. Between 1920 and 1973, for example, more than 100,000 retarded women were sterilized because of fears that they would transmit the condition to their children.[34] More recently, some authorities have attempted to bring criminal action against drug-addicted women who have given birth to addicted babies.

Since 1985 the CDC has recommended that women at risk for HIV infection "consider delaying pregnancy." That recommendation is a bit ironic since, given the course of HIV infections, a "delay" usually means that the HIV-infected woman will never be able to have a child.

The CDC's suggestion has become standard policy throughout much of the nation. Worded more or less strongly, public health statements recommend that women at risk for HIV infection not become pregnant.[35] Two physicians at the CDC, for example, included in their 1987 "AIDS Prevention

Message to the Community" the advice to women: "If you could have been exposed to HIV, get tested for antibodies; if you are positive, don't become pregnant."[36]

Some people are concerned about recommendations like these. They recognize the problem of HIV-infected babies. But they fear that the suggestions to HIV-infected women may become mandates. Such women will lose all choice in the matter. At the very least, they will feel coerced into making a decision that they may not really want to make.

Trying to convince women who are at risk for HIV infection is a very dangerous proposition, according to some authorities. After all, they point out, between 50 and 75 percent of all babies born to HIV-infected women will be healthy. This number is not so different from women whose babies are at risk for certain genetic disorders. Under these circumstances, one expert has declared that "it would represent an extraordinary invasion of privacy to forbid or prevent HIV-infected women from becoming pregnant, as much as we might want to encourage restraint."[37]

In addition, these critics see restrictions on HIV-infected women as only the beginning of further restrictions of a woman's reproductive rights. "Strongly encouraging" women with regard to HIV issues may lead to "strong encouragement" about other issues, such as genetic disorders in a fetus. As one writer has observed, such an AIDS policy reflects "[t]he beginning of an alliance between physicians and the state to force pregnant women to follow medical advice for the sake of their fetuses."[38]

Should HIV Be Added to the List of "Dangerous Contagious Diseases?" Should Immigrants and Visitors Who Are HIV+ Be Barred from Entering the Country?

In August 1987 the U.S. Congress instructed the Justice Department to add HIV infection to its list of "dangerous contagious diseases." This list is used by the Immigration and Naturalization Service (INS) to decide which individuals may enter the United States as visitors and which qualify for permanent residency and citizenship here. At one time, the list included such conditions as gonorrhea, syphilis, leprosy, and active tuberculosis.

Visitors arriving in the United States are required to demonstrate that they are not infected with any of the diseases on the list. Anyone applying for permanent residency under the 1986 Immigration Reform and Control Act is also subject to conditions of the INS list.

Objections were raised about the listing of HIV infection on the dangerous contagious disease list. Critics pointed out that HIV infection is not transmitted by casual contact. Also, the number of HIV-infected individuals who might enter the United States would be very small compared to the total number of people who are HIV+ already here. Finally, given the low risk presented by an HIV+ individual arriving in the United States, the INS policy was thought to be an unreasonable intrusion on a person's privacy.

One of the most concrete effects of listing HIV infection was the refusal of visas for foreign visitors wanting to attend the 6th International Conference on AIDS in San Francisco in June 1990. Several thousand people who did attend the conference staged a massive protest of the government's policies.

Protests were also lodged by the International Red Cross, the National Commission on AIDS, the World Health Organization, and health officials of several foreign governments. Dr. David Rogers, co-chair of the National Commission on AIDS called the listing of HIV infection a "policy that was foolish and embarrassing to the United States."[39]

In November 1990 Congress changed its mind about the listing of HIV infection. It passed an amendment declaring its previous decision void and asking Dr. Louis W. Sullivan, the secretary of Health and Human Services, to prepare a new list of dangerous contagious diseases.

Dr. Sullivan did so and, in January 1991, announced that the new list would contain only active tuberculosis. HIV infection would not be on the list. The new immigration and naturalization policy was to become effective June 1, 1991. Scientists applauded Secretary Sullivan's decision. Dr. Rogers referred to the changes as a "fine blow for science."[40]

Then, only a week before the new list was to become effective, the Bush administration changed its mind: The old list of dangerous contagious diseases would be retained, and HIV infection was to be included on the list.

The reason for the change appeared to be a massive outpouring of 40,000 letters objecting to Dr. Sullivan's January decision. Conservatives around the nation, under the leadership of Sen. Jesse Helms and Rep. William E. Dannemeyer, were apparently responsible for the deluge of letters. Representative Dannemeyer was quoted as saying that he was "pleased that H.H.S. woke up to the absurdity of this proposal, and I hope it stays buried in the bottom of a circular file in the deepest innards of the bureaucracy."[41]

That, in fact, is what may happen, at least for the near future. Government health officials admitted that they were back at "square one" and would have to "go back to the drawing board on the policy."[42]

Once again, health officials and many politicians were outraged at the administration's change of heart. Rep. Barney Frank, for example, described the action as a "perfect example of political cowardice."[43] And, faced with the continuing ban on HIV-infected people from other nations, the organizing committee for the 7th International Conference on AIDS, which was scheduled for Boston in 1992, decided to ask that the meeting be changed to some city outside of the United States.

7

AIDS and Health Workers

Most workers have no reason to fear being around someone who is HIV+. Carpenters, bankers, school teachers, auto mechanics, airline pilots, and most other workers are in no danger just because a coworker or a customer or a student is HIV+. That statement is not true for only one occupation: health care workers.

What Is the Risk That a Health Care Worker Will Acquire HIV from an Infected Patient?

Doctors, nurses, and others who work in the field of health care are exposed to risks that virtually no one else is. For example, a nurse taking blood from a patient may accidentally stick himself with the needle. A surgeon operating on a patient may cut her own finger. In such cases, the patient's blood may come into contact with that of the doctor or nurse. HIV infection is possible.

Because of their constant exposure to other people's blood, health care workers have always been regarded as a special problem in the matter of HIV testing.

This question has been thoroughly studied for more than a decade. The answer appears to be that the risk is very low. One report set the risk at 0.4 percent.[1] That is, a healthy worker who comes into contact with the blood of someone who is HIV+ stands four chances in one thousand that he or she will become infected.

That number appears remarkably low. It means that even when a person is exposed to infected blood, the risk of infection is less than 1 percent. One authority has summarized this finding by saying "the number of health care workers infected in this way is astonishingly small, demonstrating once again that AIDS is an extraordinarily difficult disease to transmit accidentally."[2]

No precise studies have been done on other means of transmission to health workers, such as exposure to infected skin or mucous membrane. But, according to one authority in the field, "well-documented cases of such transmission suggest that the level of risk [in such cases] is much lower than that associated with [exchanges of blood]."[3]

Officials from government and the health sciences have constantly tried to reassure health care workers. They acknowledge that health care workers are at greater risk for AIDS than are those in other occupations. But risk is always a part of health care, they point out. Health care workers are also at greater risk than the general public for hepatitis, tuberculosis, malaria, and any other infectious disease you can name.

The important point, authorities remind workers, is to observe standard medical procedures. Health care workers are all trained in the use of "universal precautions." This term refers to standard procedures that are followed to prevent transmission of an infection. It includes such acts as washing one's hands, wearing masks and gowns when appropriate, using care when working with needles and sharp instruments, and so on.[4]

Public health officials point out that the vast majority of HIV infections among health care workers have been the result of careless procedures by workers themselves. One writer reported, "Several workers who contracted the virus said they knew what to do to prevent infection, but for one reason or another, failed to take those simple precautions."[5]

Do Health Care Workers Have Legitimate Fears Concerning HIV Risks?

Some health care workers have not been convinced by these arguments. They point out that HIV infection is not like hepatitis or malaria. AIDS is, in most cases, fatal. If a worker becomes infected, he or she cannot begin a treatment that will cure him or her of the disease.

Besides, needle sticks and contact with blood are a common part of the medical profession. In a study by the *Annals of Internal Medicine*, nine percent of all physicians reported having been stuck with needles containing blood from an HIV+ patient.[6] At the University of California at San Francisco (UCSF), that fraction was even higher. Between 25 percent and 30 percent of all UCSF residents and interns are reported to have received needle sticks involving HIV+ blood. At San Francisco General Hospital, slightly more than half (55 percent) of all needle sticks are reported to involve blood from a high-risk individual.[7]

Because of this risk, many health care workers have asked for some means of protecting themselves from HIV infection. Sometimes their request is for what seems to be minimal protection. Four nurses at San Francisco General Hospital made such a request in 1985. They asked permission to wear gowns and masks at all times when dealing with HIV patients.[8]

Their request was denied. The wearing of gowns and masks would frighten patients, they were told. That kind of equipment is appropriate on some occasions, administrators said. But there is no medical reason for wearing it all the time.

Should All Patients Be Tested for HIV?

Another request by health care workers is that all patients be tested for HIV. That way a doctor or nurse will know which patients are infected. He or she can use special caution in working with these patients.

Probably the best known advocate of this position is Dr. Lorraine Day. Dr. Day was, until 1990, chief of orthopedic surgery at San Francisco General Hospital. During surgery, Dr. Day points out, she is often covered with blood. It is not unusual for blood to spray into her face. She has begun wearing an outfit that looks like a space suit during surgery.

Why should she be exposed to this risk, Dr. Day asks. Her life is in danger every time she operates on a patient. She deserves to know whether the person she is operating on is HIV+ or not. "There's nothing in the Hippocratic Oath," she says, "that says I have to sacrifice my life for the patient."[9]

Other doctors disagree. They reiterate that risk is part of the medical profession. When people become doctors and nurses, they know they will sometimes be in life-threatening situations. Besides, the medical profession has developed a wide range of sophisticated methods for protecting workers. The medically reasonable approach is simply for workers to treat all patients as if they were HIV+ and to use the best means available to protect themselves.

Some physicians have even questioned Dr. Day's motives. Dr. Laurens White, former president of the California Medical Association, has said that Dr. Day's extremely conservative political views are "in part . . . responsible for her attitudes toward the groups that have the infection."[10]

Furthermore, HIV testing is too unreliable to provide the information about HIV infection that some medical workers would like to have. Suppose that a patient entered a hospital shortly after being infected with HIV. Enough time might not have passed for adequate numbers of antibodies to develop in order to be detected by the ELISA test. So the patient would test negative.

But the result would be a false negative. Medical workers would have a false assurance that the patient was not infected with HIV. The workers might be in a more risky position than if they just assumed that the patient (and all patients) was HIV+.

Should Guidelines Be Written for All Health Care Workers to Follow?

Public health agencies have been trying to work out guidelines that would be fair to both physicians and patients. In 1990 the national Centers for Disease Control (CDC) suggested a policy that consisted primarily of three parts. First, all health care workers should undergo voluntary HIV testing. Second, panels of experts should be convened to decided on a case-by-case basis whether infected workers should continue to practice medicine and, if so, what kinds of procedures they could safely perform. Third, infected professionals could continue to carry out invasive procedures (those that involve the possibility of spreading the virus) only if patients are informed of the individual's HIV status ahead of time.

Some states have adopted the CDC guidelines essentially as they were written. Others have made modifications. A proposed law in New York state, for example, would not require infected health care professionals to inform patients of their HIV status. Officials believe the policy would backfire, resulting in the forced resignations of infected personnel.

As of late 1991, six states had passed laws similar to those proposed by the CDC. The most severe of those laws was enacted in Illinois. The Illinois law requires the state to notify patients of a professional's HIV status if he or she does not do so himself or herself.[11]

Should Health Care Workers Be Allowed to Refuse Treatment to Someone Who Has or Is Suspected of Being HIV+?

The most extreme way for a health care worker to avoid HIV infection is to refuse to treat an AIDS patient or someone who is known or suspected to be HIV+. A large fraction of medical workers have already indicated that they would prefer not to—or simply would not—treat anyone who is HIV+. In the *Annals of Internal Medicine* study cited earlier in the chapter, 23 percent of the doctors interviewed say that, given a choice, they would never treat an AIDS patient.

In the same survey, nearly half (42 percent) said that, given a choice, they would never treat an IV drug user whether he or she was HIV+ or not. Eleven percent said they would never knowingly treat a gay patient.

These figures suggest that fear of infection is not the only reason some medical workers want to avoid HIV+ patients. Often, they simply fear, dislike, or disapprove of gay and bisexual men and injecting drug users. In a 1988 study of doctors in Minnesota, 21 percent admitted having "moderate or great discomfort" in dealing with homosexual patients. In addition, "twenty-seven percent believed that the homosexual life-style is (or should be) unacceptable to society, and 35 percent believed that the homosexual life-style should be condemned."[12] About one in ten of the doctors surveyed expressed the belief that people who develop AIDS "deserve their disease."[13]

From time to time, specific examples of this attitude are reported in the media. For example, a young man in New York state visited his doctor in 1986 complaining of backaches. He had been seeing the doctor since 1983. The young man mentioned that he had tested positive for HIV. But he had no symptoms of AIDS.

At that point, the doctor refused to treat the young man for his back problems. He claimed that he was not qualified to treat AIDS patients. Since the patient did not yet have the disease, the point of that argument is not clear.

The director of the National Center for Bioethics wrote about the case that he "suspects the real issue, of course, is the growing fear by health care workers . . . of catching the virus from HIV-positive patients."[14]

For many individuals concerned about AIDS issues, this case highlights an important aspect of the choices facing health care workers. Those who have chosen to work in a health or medical career, they say, have a moral obligation to treat all patients, regardless of their personal feelings about the individual. A doctor, nurse, or dentist does not have the right to deny care and treatment to a patient on the basis of the person's HIV status. Such an action is an affront to one's responsibilities as a professional and as a human being.

A number of professional societies have taken official stands on this issue. The American Medical Association, for example, has stated that:

"A physician may not ethically refuse to treat a patient whose condition is within the physician's current realm of competence solely because the patient is infected with HIV."[15]

What Are the Risks of Health Care Workers Infecting Patients with HIV?

What about the risk of infection in the other direction, from health care worker to patient? For the first decade of the epidemic, no such instance was recorded. There were no known cases in which an HIV+ doctor, nurse, or other health worker passed the virus to a patient.

That record is a bit remarkable. As of January 1991, 5,815 cases of AIDS had been reported among health care workers. Of this number, 637 were physicians, 42 surgeons, 156 dental workers, and 1,199 nurses.[16] Yet, as of that date, only five cases of infection from a medical worker had been reported. All involved a single dentist in Florida who died of AIDS in late 1990.

At first authorities believed that the dentist had transmitted HIV directly to his patients. Later evidence suggested that the transmission may have occurred, at least in one case, from one patient to another because the dentist had not properly sterilized his instruments.

Almost overnight the Florida incident presented a potentially frightening new issue. What was the risk of a person's contracting HIV from his or her doctor, nurse, or dentist, people began to ask.

The American Medical Association (AMA) and the American Dental Association (ADA) responded almost immediately. Their experts calculated that the chance of acquiring HIV infection from a dentist was somewhere between 1 in 263,158 and 1 in 2,631,579. The risk of infection from a surgeon was between 1 in 41,667 and 1 in 416,667. Based on these figures, the AMA and ADA estimated that as few as 13 and as many as 128 people may have contracted the virus from a medical worker during the ten years of the epidemic.[17]

These figures were theoretical calculations and do not reflect the actual number of cases that have so far been observed. In fact, beyond the five Florida cases mentioned above, there have been no cases of health care worker to patient transmission reported.

In spite of the low rate of actual cases of transmission reported, the AMA and ADA decided to change their position on HIV infection among health workers. For the first time, both groups recommended that HIV+ health workers either inform their patients that they are infected or stop doing risky medical procedures.

Should All Health Care Workers Be Tested for HIV?

Some medical authorities suggested even more drastic measures. A Florida doctor who specializes in infectious diseases, for example, has recommended HIV testing for all health workers who come into contact with a patient's blood.[18]

Many people are enthusiastic about the AMA and ADA recommendations. They admit that the risk of infection is really very low. In comparison, for example, the risk of death in a standard anesthesia is 1 in 10,000. But people do not think in terms of numbers, they say. It is the one person who catches the virus that everyone hears about. It is that one person that no one wants to become.

Others are distressed by the AMA/ADA recommendations. They offer a number of objections. First, risk is always present in any medical situation, they say. Death during, or as a result of, some medical procedures is not uncommon; it is not on purpose, but it does happen. Figures on the risk of anesthesia support this notion.

Second, medical procedures are extremely effective at protecting patients. The fact that only five known cases of HIV infection have been contracted from a medical worker—all involving the same medical worker—confirms this view.

Many workers believe that the risk of HIV infection is much less important than other sources of infection in the field of medicine. As one nurse has said, "I can tell you about doctors who don't wash their hands between patients [a standard medical procedure]. What are we doing about that?"[19]

Third, what will happen if all HIV+ medical workers retire from the profession? By almost any estimate, thousands of doctors, nurses, dentists, and other health workers will have to give up their jobs. Can the American health care system really stand that kind of loss?

Fourth, HIV testing would be very expensive. Workers would have to be tested regularly, probably every three months. For example, the cost of testing at just one institution, San Francisco General Hospital, has been estimated at $680,000 per year. Few hospitals can really afford such a huge additional expense.[20]

Finally, health care workers, like anyone else, deserve their privacy. How can we ensure that their HIV status, if tested, could be kept confidential in a hospital?

Those who favor the AMA/ADA recommendations understand these concerns. Still, they say, a highly dangerous disease is involved. Even given all these concerns, HIV+ medical workers should either tell their patients or avoid risky medical procedures.

8

Education To Stop The Epidemic

People differ about many issues involving the AIDS epidemic. But nearly everyone is in agreement on one point: We need to stop the spread of HIV as soon as possible.

Health officials have a lot of experience in controlling infectious diseases. They know they must call on a variety of tools in order to slow down and stop an epidemic. One such tool is epidemiology. Epidemiology refers to the study of infectious diseases and how these diseases are spread throughout a community. HIV testing allows epidemiologists to find out where HIV is located in a community and how it is being spread.

Another important tool in controlling any infectious disease, including AIDS, is education. Maybe you think of schools when you hear the word education. But people become educated in a great many ways besides going to school. Radio and television, newspapers and magazines, pamphlets and brochures, bulletin boards and bumper stickers, lectures and informal discussions . . . these are just a few examples of the way education occurs in everyday life.

What Changes in Education Should Be Made to Better Explain HIV Transmission and AIDS?

One aim of AIDS educational programs is to help people avoid becoming infected with HIV. In order to do that, it is necessary to tell people how HIV is transmitted. Someone has to say, "You can get HIV in the exchange of certain body fluids."

But that statement may not be very helpful. People—especially young people—usually don't use the term "body fluids." They may not even know what it means.

Educators are tempted to use this phrase, though, because it is a polite way of saying "blood, semen, and vaginal secretions." It is difficult to tell a class that they should not "exchange blood, semen, and vaginal secretions" with someone else. Many students would not have the slightest idea how they would "exchange blood, semen, and vaginal secretions."

So the problem is this. People need to be told not to share needles with someone else and not to participate in unsafe sexual acts. They need to learn that HIV can be transmitted through unprotected vaginal, anal, and oral sex. But that is a difficult message. Many people do not want to talk about injecting drug use or sex in any form.

For example, an effective method for protecting against HIV infection is for a man to wear a condom during sexual intercourse. Think what an effective educational tool it would be for all television stations to carry this message. They could provide a public service message about condoms, as they do for health organizations such as the American Cancer Society.

Or they could allow condom manufacturers to advertise, as they allow the manufacturers of vaginal sprays and other personal health products to advertise. In doing so, they could probably make a major contribution to AIDS education.

To date, however, no major television network has allowed either a public service announcement or a commercial message about condom use. Networks claim that they will offend viewers with information about condoms.

Critics admit that some people will be offended by condom advertisements. But surveys show the number who will object is no greater than the number who already object to the advertising of tampons, vaginal sprays, and other personal products. In its 1988 report on AIDS, sexual behavior, and drug use, the National Research Council strongly recommended that national television networks reverse their policies on condom advertising. It recommended that "television networks present more public service messages on those behaviors associated with HIV transmission and . . . accept condom advertisements."[1]

What Role Should the Government Have in AIDS Education?

That question has been debated on a national, state, and local levels for over a decade. On the one hand, at least part of the answer appears seem to be obvious. Educating the general public about health issues is one function of the U.S. Public Health Service and state and local health departments. However, during the first half decade of the epidemic, there appeared to be relatively little concern about AIDS education at the federal level and, in many cases, at state and local levels.

In reviewing previous governmental educational efforts in 1985, the Office of Technology Assessment concluded that "So far, efforts to prevent AIDS through education have received minimal funding, especially efforts targeted at groups at highest risk."[2] A year and a half later, a report by the National Academy of Science's Institute of Medicine found little progress. The report pointed out how critical educational programs are in stopping the spread of AIDS. It then expressed dismay at the "woefully inadequate" efforts made by the federal government during the first five years of the epidemic.[3]

Do Politics Hinder the Government's Ability to Explain HIV Transmission and AIDS to Americans?

Governmental agencies at a state and local level were largely ineffective also. One problem was the legal status of people who were most afflicted by the disease—gay men. Homosexual acts are illegal in twenty-four states and the District of Columbia. How can a state or local health department teach gay men about safe sex when the behaviors it would be describing are criminal acts in many states?

An example of this problem—at the federal level—occurred in the fall of 1987. The United States Senate was considering a bill to fund various health care projects. Senator Jesse Helms of North Carolina proposed an amendment to the bill. The amendment would prohibit the spending of any federal money on "AIDS education, information, or prevention materials and activities that promote or encourage, directly or indirectly, homosexual activities."[4]

Helms had become angry when shown a Gay Men's Health Crisis comic book on safe sex. He said the book was "so obscene that it nearly made him 'throw up.' " He acknowledged that federal funds had not been used in producing the book. But GMHC did receive federal funds for other activities. He was outraged that GMHC was apparently using federal money for the "promotion of sodomy."[5]

Helms' position was a surprise to no one. He has been quite vocal in attacking gay-related activities in the United States. What was surprising was the nearly unanimous support his amendment received from his colleagues. The amendment passed by a vote of 94-2 in the Senate and 368-47 in the House of Representatives.

90

Should the Government Send Out Pamphlets to Every Household in America Explaining HIV Transmissions and AIDS?

Controversy also surrounded a second major effort by the federal government to promote AIDS education. In October 1986, Surgeon General C. Everett Koop issued a report on the AIDS epidemic. The report had been eagerly awaited by everyone who had an interest in the disease. Dr. Koop was a 70-year-old pediatrician with a well-known conservative philosophy. He had taken strong stands against abortion, for example. Many people—including members of the Reagan administration—hoped that Dr. Koop would use his report to criticize the lifestyles of people who had been affected by the epidemic.

But they were disappointed in that expectation. Dr. Koop acknowledged that "some Americans have difficulties with the subjects of sex, sexual practices, and alternative lifestyles. Many Americans are opposed to homosexuality, promiscuity of any kind, and prostitution." But, he insisted, discussion of the epidemic had to go on entirely from "a health and medical point of view."[6]

His report clearly explained what AIDS is, how HIV infection occurs, and how it can and cannot be transmitted. The surgeon general placed special emphasis on the need for education to stop the epidemic. He insisted, "Education concerning AIDS must start at the lowest grade possible as part of any health and hygiene program." He emphasized that such classes should focus on "the prevention of AIDS and other sexually transmitted diseases."[7]

A number of national figures were outraged at Dr. Koop's approach to AIDS. He should have emphasized the moral aspects of the disease, they said. He should have explained how certain lifestyles were responsible for HIV infection.

Congressman William E. Dannemeyer of California wrote Koop about his feelings. He claimed that public health authorities should not teach just about the medical aspects of AIDS. They should also explain the "moral and ethical reasons which exist for avoiding homosexuality." He accused Dr. Koop of ignoring or denying "the heterosexual ethic which is the foundation of our civilization."[8]

Objections to Dr. Koop's approach to the AIDS epidemic were soon to rise again. Koop announced plans to send copies of an eight-page pamphlet to every household in the nation. In the summer of 1987, Congress appropriated $20 million for this project. Like the surgeon general's report, the pamphlet was to present straightforward scientific information about the causes of AIDS and how the disease is transmitted.

Before it could be published, however, the pamphlet went through an extensive series of reviews in other government agencies. Some of those agencies had a considerably different view about AIDS education than did the surgeon general.[9]

Eventually, in September 1987, Assistant Secretary of Health Robert Windom announced a change of plans. The White House was concerned about some information in the pamphlet, he said. Although 45 million copies had already been printed, a decision had been made to delay its distribution. Instead, the new plan was to send the pamphlet to health departments, community organizations, and major employers.[10]

Now it was the turn of some members of Congress to be outraged. They pointed out that they had specifically allocated $20 million for the pamphlet project. Under this pressure, Secretary Windom changed his mind. In early 1988, a new version of the AIDS pamphlet, "Understanding AIDS," was mailed to 107 million households in the United States.

Some congressmen felt as strongly about "Understanding AIDS" as Rep. Dannemeyer had about the surgeon general's report. Rep. Jim Bunning of Kentucky, for example, sent a special mailing to 200,000 households in his district. Under a bright red "ALERT" warning, he told his constituents that the pamphlet suggested that "abnormal sexual activity is acceptable if one takes certain precautions." Similar warning were sent out by Rep. Richard Baker and Rep. Jim McCrery, both of Louisiana.[11]

How successful was the pamphlet as an educational tool? That is a difficult question to answer. On the one hand, it produced more than 250,000 telephone calls to a special hotline number listed in the pamphlet. And, according to one survey, 74 percent of those who received the pamphlet read all or part of it.[12]

On the other hand, another survey found that only 19 percent of those who were questioned had read any part of the pamphlet "carefully." Nearly half said that they did not read the pamphlet because it never arrived (29 percent) or they chose not to read it (16 percent).[13]

What Does the Term Militant Activism Mean? Should AIDS Activists Engage in Civil Disobedience?

Some people long ago lost patience with the way in which government agencies and corporations have dealt with the AIDS epidemic. They believed that established bureaucracies have worked too slowly. They have argued that lives are being lost unnecessarily while "business as usual" goes on in laboratories and legislative chambers.

Perhaps the best known organization to espouse these views is ACT-UP. ACT-UP is an abbreviation for AIDS Coalition to Unleash Power. The members of ACT-UP believe that working with and through the political system is not an effective way to deal with the HIV crisis.

They argue that militant confrontation is the best way to get people's attention and bring about change. This philosophy is illustrated by the group's slogan, "AIDS = Genocide; Silence = Death; Fight Back!" By 1991 ACT-UP had more than sixty chapters nationwide.

Some of the actions sponsored by ACT-UP have included blocking San Francisco's Golden Gate Bridge during a morning commute, disrupting opening night at the San Francisco Opera, sitting-in during mass at New York City's St. Patrick Cathedral, blocking the offices of Burroughs-Wellcome Pharmaceutical, demonstrating in front of New York City's city hall, closing down the Food and Drug Administration headquarters for a day in 1988, and shouting down Secretary of Health and Human Services Louis Sullivan at the 1990 International AIDS Conference in San Francisco.

Members of ACT-UP argue that they are carrying on an American tradition: civil disobedience. Politicians seldom attack discrimination and social injustice on their own, out of the goodness of their hearts, they say. Social reform comes when people demand it. Every important reform movement from the suffrage movement to the civil rights movement confirms that fact, they point out. More money for AIDS research and education and an end to discrimination against people with AIDS will come only when someone like ACT-UP demands these changes.

Officials admit that ACT-UP has been effective. The organization has forced government and the public to confront the AIDS epidemic. More liberal federal policies on drug tests, for example, resulted at least in part because of ACT-UP's efforts.[14]

People outside the AIDS movement have also been impressed by the methods and successes of AIDS activists, especially those of ACT-UP. Abbey Meters, executive director of the National Organization of Rare Disorders, has said that "AIDS patients have accomplished so much through civil disobedience, and we know of many organizations that work for diseases that are just as deadly and just as horrible. They are saying: 'Maybe we should go down to Washington and block traffic.' "[15]

But a number of people are disturbed by ACT-UP's tactics. Many members of the gay community, for example, are embarrassed by the group's outrageous behaviors. They say that those behaviors create too much ill will. The organization does more harm than good, they say.

Members of the general public are often upset by ACT-UP also. For example, a number of commuters were very angry at the Golden Gate Bridge blockade. Some vowed that they would no longer support AIDS organizations and activities because they had been inconvenienced.[16]

ACT-UP's work renews a long debate in American political life. How far can and should people go to bring about political change. Every important civil rights movement has debated that question. Blacks who fought for civil rights were said to be "uppity." Women who sought the right to vote were called "mannish" and "mentally unstable." Gays who are fighting discrimination today may be labeled as troublemakers.

Yet without strong, often disruptive protests, would many types of social reform in the United States ever have taken place? That is the question members of ACT-UP ask and about which its opponents debate.

Should Needle Exchange Programs Be Allowed so that Injecting Drug Users Lower the Risks of Getting or Passing HIV?

Education programs for injecting drug users contain one critical element: teaching individuals about the risks of using dirty needles and of sharing needles. According to some studies, 85 percent or more of drug users share needles.[17] Slowing the spread of HIV among drug users will depend heavily, therefore, on dealing with this problem.

Some state and local governments have printed pamphlets warning users not to share needles. In other places, health workers, recovered addicts, and private citizens have carried this message into the streets.

Ideally, of course, the objective of these campaigns might be to help addicts stop using drugs entirely. But that goal is seldom achieved. Many addicts have no motivation to give up drugs. Those who do often have great difficulty getting into rehabilitation programs. So, while they would like to help users "kick their habit," many workers do not believe this is a realistic, short-term goal.

The next best step, some people believe, is to make sure that addicts use only clean needles. In some communities, educational programs are keyed to teach users how to clean their needles with bleach. The bleach destroys HIV and makes the needles safe (at least from an HIV standpoint) to use.

The most ambitious and controversial programs for reducing HIV infection among drug users provide for needle exchanges. In these programs, a drug user turns in all the needles he or she has used during a week. In exchange, that person receives an equal number of new, clean needles.

Needle exchange programs have been set up—usually illegally and unofficially—in cities as diverse as New York City; San Francisco; Seattle; Portland, Oregon; Tacoma, Washington; Boulder, Colorado; Edinburgh, Scotland; and Zurich, Switzerland.

The argument for these programs is fairly straightforward. Drug users will not transmit HIV with clean needles. They may with dirty needles. The more users use clean needles rather than dirty needles, the less HIV infection there will be in the community.

There are, however, a number of objections to needle exchange programs. In the first place, drug use is illegal in all states. Providing users with needles constitutes a criminal act. Perhaps drug laws should be changed, some people say. But right now needle exchange programs are simply against the law.

Others object to needle exchange programs because, they say, such programs send the wrong message. They tell users that it is okay to use drugs. HIV infection is an epidemic, to be sure. But so is drug use. You don't stop the drug use problem by providing users with the tools they need (needles).

Opposition to needle exchange programs is especially strong among blacks. Drug use has historically been regarded as more of a problem in the black than the non-black community.[18] Some black leaders believe that needle exchange programs only encourage drug addiction. To the extent that they do, they only increase one of the black community's most serious problems.

"We have communities and families and churches that are under siege by drug addicts" is the way the Reverend Amos Brown of San Francisco's Third Baptist Church puts it. "And we've got to put a stop to this. And you don't stop a fire by putting more fire on it."[19]

A similar view was expressed by LuLann McGriff, chairwoman of the western region of the National Association for the Advancement of Colored People. Needle exchange, she claimed, "fosters drug use and is another form of genocide. Experiment on somebody else," she said. "We don't want it."[20]

San Francisco's mayor, Dianne Feinstein, also expressed her disapproval. "In my opinion," the mayor said, "it is a terrible and truly offensive idea, which would put the health department in the position of aiding and abetting drug addiction . . . How can we consider spending the public's money for drug paraphernalia?"[21]

Research studies have begun to show that needle exchange programs do not contribute to drug addiction problems. They appear to suggest that such programs do reduce the number of needles that are shared without increasing drug use among addicts.[22]

President George Bush also holds a dim view of needle exchange programs. In July 1989 he declared that he is opposed to such programs "under any circumstances."[23]

As of May 1991, only about a quarter of the American public believed that needle exchange programs would be a "very effective" way to fight AIDS. However, twice that number thought that needle exchange programs were probably going to occur anyway.[24]

The concerns of people opposed to needle exchange programs are easy to understand. But if such programs are not the answer, what is? As one black woman in San Francisco's needle exchange program has said, "This is something that has to be done. . . [Addicts] are out there. They're using these needles. They're sharing them. I think it's genocide to sit back and let them."[25]

Should Condoms Be Given Away Free to Young People? Should Condoms Be Given Away in Schools?

One way to avoid HIV infection is not to engage in sexual activity and never to use injecting drugs. Many people believe that this is the message that adults should be giving to young people. Many members of the Reagan administration, for example, believed that this message should be the main theme of any pamphlets printed by the federal government.[26]

The problem is that some young women and men will not remain abstinent (without sexual activity). For these people, perhaps the best way to avoid HIV infection is by using condoms.

For this reason, many sex educators recommend teaching young people about condoms. They may also recommend that condoms be freely available to any person who wants them. The logic is that many youngsters are, in any case, going to be sexually active. If they know about condoms and have them available, they will be less likely to contract or pass on HIV.

That was the line of thinking in the health department at California's Mt. Tamalpais High School in 1990. The department announced that it would begin giving away condoms to any student who asked for them.

Many teachers, parents, and townspeople were very angry when they heard this announcement. They strongly opposed the school's handing out condoms. To do so, they said, would only encourage students to become sexually active. Boys and girls who never thought of having sex would be inspired to do so by the giveaway program, they argued. In the end, the school backed down. It canceled its planned condom giveaway program.

Other school districts are still debating the condom giveaway issue. In one district, the nation's largest, the issue has apparently been resolved. In February 1991 the New York City Board of Education voted to start a condom giveaway program in about thirty of its high schools. Eventually, the program is to be expanded to all 120 high schools.[27]

This decision has not met with unanimous approval, of course. Opposition to the plan has been led by the Roman Catholic Cardinal of New York, John O'Connor. The church's position was that the condom giveaway program would only encourage immoral behavior among the youth of New York City.[28]

But the plan did receive the support of a wide array of local institutions. Private foundations in the city agreed to pay for the cost of the program. Local hospitals said they would help schools develop AIDS prevention programs. At least two condom makers offered to contribute free condoms to the program. And the American Foundation for AIDS Research agreed to provide teams of professionals for each of the schools in the program.[29]

In the fall of 1991, the San Francisco School District followed the lead of New York City. It decided to make condoms available in all sixteen city high schools beginning in the spring of 1992.

Should Special Education Programs Be Aimed at Women, Minorities, and Young People? If so, What Type of Education Should Be Used?

The changing face of the AIDS epidemic was described in Chapter 3. Those changes suggest that the focus of educational programs in the 1990s will have to broaden to include groups that were largely ignored in the 1980s: women, minorities, children and adolescents, and the homeless. In many cases, members of these groups were missed by educational efforts that were aimed at gay and bisexual men and injecting drug users.

New educational programs will have to take into consideration certain special characteristics of each group. For example, women have often been taught that they should be care-givers. As wives and mothers, their role has usually been to provide comfort. HIV infection means that a woman must adopt a new role—that of one who receives care and comfort.

Women   One booklet for women with HIV infection reminds readers, "We have often put other people's needs ahead of our own. But as a women with HIV infection, you are now in need of care and attention from others."[30]

Also, women in this society (and in nearly all societies) tend to be in a subordinate role in both personal and social settings. Avoiding HIV infection means taking strong, positive action in both sexual and drug situations. For example, a woman may have to insist that a man wear a condom during sexual intercourse.

But many women may lack the assertiveness to take such actions. In a statement concerning the issue of women and HIV infection, five professional scientists wrote that "it is unclear that women, given their relative lack of power in sexual and drug-using relationships, will be able to assert themselves and insist on protective behaviors."[31]

Other writers have made similar observations. A writer in *Ebony* magazine, for example, claims that "[o]ftentimes, women feel the need to practice safe sex, but are not prepared to deal with reprisals from male partners who don't wish to use condoms."[32]

Women tend to have less economic and social influence also. This fact is especially true for women of color, poor women, and women who have been abused. A pamphlet prepared for women with HIV infection warns that "[i]t is sometimes hard to be heard by people who lead a life very different from your own." But then it also advises readers to "[k]eep asking your questions and looking for the services you need. You have real needs that should be met. Don't give up!"[33]

In some respects, an educational program about AIDS for women is not so different from one for men. One important difference, however, is the way the program is presented. Women are beginning to speak to women about HIV infection. They are learning to work together to educate and provide support for each other.

Minorities Educational programs for blacks and other minorities must also face certain realities. For example, some of the behaviors that lead to HIV infection—homosexual behavior and drug use, for example—are regarded with very strong disapproval in the black and other minority communities. Many individuals in such communities have found it difficult to talk about AIDS and HIV infections because of these taboos.[34]

Changes are beginning to occur in some minority communities, however. For example, some black churches are beginning to provide educational programs about AIDS. Some present information in sermons or in the weekly church bulletin. Others have established support groups for people with AIDS and people who are HIV+.

AIDS programs for minorities face yet another problem: cost. With a disproportionate number of poor people in their communities, many black, Hispanics, and other minorities believe that they can not afford to pay for the expensive treatments that HIV infections may require.

Finally, as terrible as HIV infection is, some minority communities believe that other problems are more serious. Some Native American communities, for example, are just beginning to appreciate the threat posed by AIDS and HIV infection. For many years, these communities have been battling terrible poverty, unemployment, and alcoholism. Many Native Americans believed that AIDS was just not important enough to deserve any of the limited energy that people had for dealing with social problems. As more communities see individuals who are HIV+ appearing within them, some of these attitudes are slowly beginning to change.

Young People The task of educating adolescents about HIV infections presents some unique challenges. For one thing, adolescents are going through a difficult period of their lives. They are just beginning to understand their own personalities and their own sexualities. The period is one of "raging hormones" that sometimes make rational discussion of sexual issues difficult.

The problem is especially severe for those individuals who engage in same-sex sexual behavior or who identify themselves as gay. Such individuals may find it extremely difficult to talk about the kinds of behaviors that may lead to HIV infection. Yet, as one authority has said, "[i]t is impossible to learn safe behavior without talking about risky behavior."[35]

Another challenge for those who work with adolescents is the concept of immortality that many teenagers have. Many young men and women appear to find it hard to believe that they will ever die. So discussions of life-threatening behaviors—like those that result in HIV infection—may not be taken seriously by some adolescents.

Today, a large majority of Americans agree that AIDS education for youngsters is an important step in stopping the spread of the disease. By 1988, 94 percent of parents questioned in a survey agreed that AIDS education should be offered by schools.[36]

But what kind of AIDS education should be provided and for whom? It is one thing to talk to gay men about the dangers of anal sex. But how do you deliver the same message to an eighth-grade boy? Or should you even try to deliver that message? If not, what do you say about AIDS to young people?

Such questions are at the heart of AIDS education issues. Most people support the notion that the AIDS epidemic should be brought under control. But how do you teach about HIV and AIDS without mentioning lifestyles, acts, and practices that are despicable to many Americans?

Schools have not yet found the answer to these questions. Many large, urban school systems have already introduced AIDS education programs. But, in general, these programs tend to be short and not very specific.[37]

Experts continue to recommend that AIDS education be started as early as possible, certainly before children become sexually active. The aims of these programs, according to a National Research Council study, should be to:

1. Calm fears in elementary school

2. Teach about sexual transmission of HIV in junior high school

3. Introduce the subjects of homosexual and heterosexual behaviors, decision-making, and the use of contraceptives in senior high school.[38]

Runaway teenagers present additional problems. Most young men and women who have left home are not in school or accessible to many traditional forms of AIDS education. They are likely to be too frightened to go to HIV testing centers. Or they may lack the financial resources to get regular health care. Furthermore, a large number of homeless teenagers are involved in prostitution and drug use, which places them at risk for HIV infection. By one estimate, 15 percent of homeless youth in San Francisco are HIV+.[39]

Finding ways to tailor AIDS education programs to the previously forgotten groups of women, minorities, and youth is one of the great challenges facing health educators in the 1990s.

9

Research And Funding

Education is not a cure for the disease. Only medical research can find a way to finally bring this disease under control.

Medical research on AIDS has two goals: (1) to find drugs that will kill the AIDS virus and that can be used to treat AIDS-related diseases and (2) to develop a vaccine against HIV infection. Achieving the first goal will provide a way of helping people who have already been infected with HIV. Reaching the second goal will offer a way of protecting people against HIV infections in the future.

Can Research Stop AIDS?

There are many steps along the way to accomplishing these goals. First, scientists have to learn a great deal more about the immune system. They also need to understand the AIDS virus much better. These kinds of research are a form of basic research. Basic research provides new information about some part of nature (such as the human immune system or the nature of viruses) even though that information may have no immediate, practical value. Basic research provides the groundwork on which all other forms of research are based.

Scientists also have to solve a number of practical problems involving HIV. How can you test for the virus? How is the virus transmitted? What chemicals can be used to kill the virus? What kind of vaccine will protect the immune system against the virus? Questions like these are examples of applied research. They are questions that involve practical problems in the real world.

Quite often, funding for basic research comes from the government. The public pays for this kind of research through its tax dollars. Private companies generally say that they cannot afford to pay for research that has no immediate use. Instead, they usually concentrate on applied research. They attempt to develop products, such as drugs, that they can market and sell. The sale of these products pays for the research originally needed to develop the products.

Should More Funding Be Given to AIDS Research?

From an economic standpoint, the first case of AIDS appeared in the United States at just the wrong time. Ronald Reagan had been elected president in 1980. He brought to Washington a conservative philosophy. That philosophy meant, among other things, a belief in reducing government expenses and government services.

Reagan's first full year in office, 1981, saw not only the first cases of AIDS reported but also massive cuts in the budgets of many government agencies. The 1981 budget for the national Centers for Disease Control (CDC), for example, was cut by 25 percent and that of the Food and Drug Administration, was cut by 30 percent.[1]

In addition, many conservatives in the administration and the legislature had less than compassionate feelings for people afflicted with HIV infection.

It is hardly surprising, then, to learn that the federal government provided only minimal funding for HIV research in the first few years of the epidemic.

Total AIDS funding in 1982, for example, amounted to $5.5 million. Three years later, that amount had grown to $96 million. That increase may sound impressive. However, it should be viewed in perspective. In 1985, for comparison, the National Institutes of Health had a total budget of over $3 billion. Thus, AIDS spending accounted for less than 1 percent of the agency's overall budget.[2]

One might also compare this level of funding to that for other medical emergencies. In 1976, for example, the nation was threatened by a severe flu epidemic. The government spent $135 million to develop a national immunization program to meet that threat. Even in the third year of the HIV epidemic, the government was spending only about three-quarters of that amount on AIDS research.[3]

The interesting point is that even this modest level of funding was made possible only because of the vigorous efforts of a few legislators. Government health officials appeared unaware of and/or unconcerned about the epidemic. As California Congresswoman Barbara Boxer has said, "It was the strangest thing. Normally in an epidemic, health officials come begging Congress for more money. It seemed that we had to beg them to say they needed it."[4]

Health administrators in the early 1980s apparently thought that they really did not need more money. President Reagan at first suggested that AIDS research be paid for out of the general health budget. Even the Secretary of the Department of Health and Human Services, Margaret Heckler, fought against increased AIDS funding. "I really don't think there is another dollar that would make a difference," she said in 1983.[5]

At the moment she made that statement, however, the CDC research laboratories could not afford to buy the test tubes they needed, nor could they afford to hire the new staff needed to do AIDS research.[6]

The Tide Turns

After 1985, patterns of government funding began to change rapidly. The AIDS budget reached $61.5 million in 1984. Then it began to grow rapidly every year over the next four years. By 1990, the total budget for AIDS research and education had reached $1.6 billion. That amount was the fourth largest spent by the government on any disease.[7]

One factor, of course, is increased awareness about the disease. People in every part of government have gradually come to recognize the terrible nature of HIV infection. They now realize the threat it poses to many Americans. Even Secretary Heckler eventually acknowledged this point. In 1983 she reported to Congress that AIDS was the Department of Health and Human Services' "highest priority emergency health problem."[8]

Another factor contributing to increased AIDS funding, however, was the work of grass-roots AIDS organizations. At first, these groups were composed largely of gay men. Before long, however, they expanded to include a wide array of individuals from many different backgrounds.

The gay men who worked within the first AIDS organizations were not unfamiliar with the political process. Many had been working for years trying to influence legislative and executive actions on gay rights issues. Partly as a result of this background, AIDS organizations quickly became skilled at convincing decision-makers at all levels of government about the need for increased funding for AIDS-related activities.

Politicians were forced to realize that AIDS was no longer a health problem affecting a small minority of Americans whom they could ignore. It had become a major health crisis that affected a broad range of their constituents.

How Much Funding for AIDS Research Would Be Too Much?

The early 1990s saw yet another change in the pattern of AIDS funding. Some people began to question the constantly increasing AIDS budget. Should we expect those involved in AIDS research and education to expect twice as much money every year for their work, some people asked.

As early as 1988 conservative columnist James J. Kilpatrick had asked, "Aren't we overreacting to AIDS?"[9] Why should AIDS research get so much more attention than other medical problems, he asked. Recently, another editorialist has called AIDS "the most privileged disease in America."[10]

One reason for this new attitude about AIDS funding was the belief by some observers that the epidemic was slowing down. The main spokesperson for that viewpoint has been Michael Fumento. Fumento has argued that the tide has begun to turn in the AIDS epidemic. The rate of new HIV infections has begun to decrease. In his 1990 book, *The Myth of Heterosexual AIDS*, Fumento refers to AIDS as "the incredible shrinking epidemic."[11]

Many agencies have begun to lower their estimate of the number of new AIDS cases in the future, Fumento points out. And the fear that HIV would begin to spread through the heterosexual community in the United States has proved to be false. If the spread of HIV is beginning to slow down, Fumento argues, then research funding can begin to drop back.[12]

More to the point, critics say, AIDS is already getting more than its fair share of health research money. AIDS funding in 1990 exceeded that for all other diseases except cancer, genetic diseases, and heart disease. Yet AIDS causes only a fraction of the deaths caused by many other diseases. In one year, less than 100,000 people die of AIDS. But five times that number die of cancer and ten times the number die from heart disease.[13]

The result, some observers argue, is that health financing is grossly unfair. In 1990 the CDC spent an average of $10,000 on research and education for each person with AIDS. In contrast, it spent an average of $185 for each cancer patient and $3.50 for each cardiac patient.[14] Where is the justice in that kind of funding pattern, they ask?

Medical researchers themselves often support this view. In a 1990 poll of 148 scientists, nearly half believed that too much money was being spent on AIDS research. Those who work on cancer research are sometimes especially bitter. Dr. Vincent T. DeVita, former director of the National Cancer Institute, has complained that AIDS "has been an extraordinary drain on the energy of the scientific establishment."[15] And Dr. Robert Young, president of the American Society of Clinical Oncology, has said that "the superstructure of cancer research is being dismantled" because of the imbalance in medical research funding.[16]

What Are the Different Views on Funding?

The demand for reduced spending on AIDS has certainly not been unanimous. In early 1991, for example, a panel of experts created by the Institute of Medicine called for a large increase in funding for AIDS research. The panel believed that President Bush's recommended increase of 6 percent for 1992 was not enough. An increase of 25 percent was what was really needed, it said.[17]

Supporters of increased AIDS funding present a number of points to support their view. First, many authorities believe that the AIDS epidemic is not leveling off. They point out that the number of HIV infections is still increasing each year. According to one estimate, the number of new AIDS cases will triple between 1990 and 1993.[18] As a result, doctors could be treating more than a million AIDS patients during the 1990s.

Also, many authorities are still concerned about the spread of HIV among heterosexuals. For example, at one point early in the epidemic, the ratio of male to female carriers of HIV was eleven to one. Today, it is close to three to one. In some rural areas of the United States, the ratio has nearly reached one to one.[19]

An argument can also be made that AIDS is especially devastating to society because it is a disease of the young. More than four out of five of those who die from AIDS are under the age of forty-four. Think of the lost productivity caused by all those deaths, they say.

Research on AIDS is also defended because of the knowledge it can provide about the immune system, viruses, cancer, and other medical topics. Dr. June E. Osborn, dean of the University of Michigan School of Public Health, has said that AIDS research has already produced "many broadly important facts about how the body works." Also, she points out, this research has provided "more spin-offs for cancer and other diseases than for AIDS directly."[20]

Finally, one cannot assume that "extra" money now being spent on AIDS research could or would go to other health projects. The money might just not be appropriated at all. Or it might go to defense or social programs or somewhere else. William F. Raub, acting director of the National Institutes of Health, thinks that "surplus" AIDS funding would probably not have gone to cancer or genetic diseases or heart research. "Most likely," he says, "it would have been used elsewhere in the federal budget."[21]

Critics of AIDS funding see flaws in all these arguments. They admit that many young people die of AIDS. But other diseases also kill young people. As Michael Fumento has said, "[e]very year cancer and heart disease *each* kills more than 150,000 Americans below the age of sixty, while this year AIDS will kill around 30,000 persons of all ages."[22] (As you can see, there is some dispute as to what people mean when they say "young": "under forty-four" to some and "below the age of sixty" to others.)

Also, not everyone is convinced about the value of spin-offs from AIDS research. Fumento has argued that "In fact, no life has ever been saved, no disease ever ameliorated, by AIDS spin-offs."[23]

Besides, he says, we should spend money directly on problems we want to solve, not hope for spin-offs from other areas. "If it is a cure for cancer we seek," he writes, "we should spend money on cancer research, not on another disease entirely."[24]

Fumento, in turn, has had his own critics. One reviewer of *The Myth of Heterosexual AIDS* called the book "insidious." He said that Fumento presents "what is otherwise a legitimate and soundly reasoned thesis." But the author damages his argument, the reviewer goes on, by displaying a "seeming (and unseemly) callousness toward AIDS victims" that leaves the reader believing that Fumento may not be "so sure that AIDS is really such a bad thing."[25]

Other reviewers criticized Fumento for using "an insidiously homophobic, flippant style to heighten an 'us versus them' attitude toward the crisis" and called *The Myth of Heterosexual AIDS* a "dishonest book" that offered a "Reagan administration apologia for its cruel and often malevolent indifference to an American epidemic."[26]

How Successful Has the Search Been for AIDS Drugs?

A major goal of AIDS research is to find drugs that can be used against the disease. How successful has that effort been? The answer to that question depends on whom you ask.

Some medical researchers are impressed by how much has been learned about HIV in only a decade of research. They point out that two antiviral drugs (drugs that kill a virus)—AZT and ddI—have already been developed, tested, and put into use. Other antiviral drugs—dideoxycytidine, or ddC, is one example—are moving closer to approval. Many more drugs are available for AIDS-related disorders.

Many people believe, however, that the development of new AIDS drugs is moving too slowly. One problem is simply the process by which new drugs are approved for use in the United States. The agency responsible for that process is the Food and Drug Administration (FDA). Before approving a drug for commercial use, the FDA must be convinced that it both safe and effective. Drug companies are required to submit extensive research evidence to show that a new medicine will act as it is supposed to act without harming a person.

The most common form of drug testing involves two groups of people. One group, the experimental group, receives the drug being tested. The second group, the control group, receives a placebo, a harmless substance, such as starch. The health of the two groups is compared. Based on that comparison, a researcher can tell what effects, if any, the experimental drug had.

The drug approval process today is very lengthy. First the drug has to be developed in the laboratory. Then it has to be tested on experimental animals, such as rats or mice. Finally, it has to be tested again with humans. Only when these steps have been completed will the FDA consider approving the drug. That process today may take anywhere from seven to ten years.

On rare occasions, the FDA will speed up that process. A drug may show great promise while it is still in the testing stage. At that point, the FDA may declare the drug an investigational new drug and may allow release of the drug under special circumstances.

AZT and ddI fell into this category. Researchers realized how effective they were during the testing phase. They suggested that the drugs be approved for use even before the tests had been completed. On this basis, AZT received the fastest evaluation and approval the FDA had ever granted.[27]

What Are the Economics of Drug Research?

Many HIV+ people still think that drug companies and the FDA are not doing enough. They complain that too little money is being spent on drug research. How do drug companies and the FDA respond to these criticisms?

In actual fact, relatively few drug manufacturers are interested in working on AIDS drugs. Developing a new drug often costs many millions of dollars. The process may take eighteen months before the drug is even ready for testing. Testing may then take another five years or more.

That amount of time and money is worth it only if the company can eventually make a profit on the drug. Suppose that there are less than 100,000 people with AIDS in the United States. That may seem like a large number of customers for the new drug. But remember how much money the company has invested in the drug's development. It may have to charge a very high price for the drug.

When AZT was first released, it cost $8,000 to $10,000 for a year's supply of the medicine. Burroughs-Wellcome, the drug's manufacturer, said the price was necessary in order for the company to earn a profit on the drug.

But critics pointed out that many people with AIDS simply could not afford to pay that much for a drug. Even with the help of private insurers and government agencies, the cost of AZT was thought to be much too high. In response to this concern, Burroughs-Wellcome eventually reduced the cost of AZT to about half its original price.

For this reason many drug companies have chosen not to do research on AIDS drugs. They prefer to spend their time and money on health problems with a larger market. For example, think of all the allergy sufferers in the world. Development of a new allergy medicine would produce much larger profits than would a new AIDS drug.

Companies have other reasons to avoid working on AIDS drugs. For example, there is always the danger of a lawsuit. For one person in a thousand, a new drug may not work as it was intended to. A single lawsuit can wipe out all a company's profits on a new drug.

Also, companies worry about bad publicity. Consider the case with Burroughs-Wellcome. Some people say the company should be praised for developing AZT. Others complain that Burroughs-Wellcome moved too slowly on AZT and charges too much for its product. They say that Burroughs-Wellcome is making a huge profit on people's suffering. Other drug companies do not want to become involved in that kind of controversy.

For all these reasons, research on new AIDS drugs may be going on in a relatively small number of drug companies. The result is that the development of new drugs may also be progressing more slowly than it could.

Is the New Drug Approval Too Slow? What Alternative Drug Therapies Exist?

One of the problems that has most annoyed people with AIDS is what they see as the slow process of drug development and approval. Over and over again, gay newspapers and other periodicals interested in AIDS issues have carried reports of new drugs that might be effective against HIV. Sometimes these drugs have been experimental compounds developed by scientists. Other times, they have been herbs, natural products, and other materials from outside traditional medical research.

An organization called Project Inform has been created to tell people with AIDS about these alternative methods of treatment. Project Inform publishes a newsletter, *AIDS Treatment News*, that summarizes and describes alternative therapies and drugs for use against HIV.[28]

Normally, however, these alternative drugs have not been available to people with AIDS. The FDA has forbidden their release until they have been tested and found to be effective and safe. That policy is unacceptable to many people with AIDS. After all, they would probably all be dead by the time the approval process had been completed on some or all of these drugs.

Nonetheless, in the early years of the AIDS epidemic, the FDA insisted on this policy. The agency could not allow people to use untested drugs, it said. Those drugs might cause serious health problems for anyone who took them. They might even cause the deaths of individuals.

People with AIDS rejected that argument. They were, after all, dying. Should they not have the chance to take anything that might prolong their lives or make them feel better? Were they not entitled to the freedom of choice as to which drugs they thought might help them?[29]

Following up on this philosophy, many people with AIDS have tried dozens of untested, unapproved drugs in an effort to improve their health and save their lives. The fact that their actions were illegal has been essentially irrelevant to these actions.

In July 1988 the FDA changed its policy on alternative drug use by people with AIDS. It decided to allow those individuals to import and use drugs that had not been officially approved by the FDA.

Later the FDA made even more changes in its drug testing and use policies. For example, it approved the previously unofficial test of a drug known as Compound Q. Compound Q is obtained from a Chinese plant that belongs to the cucumber family. Some people with AIDS have taken Compound Q and found that it was effective. At least, they thought that their health had improved as a result of taking the drug.

In 1989, members of Project Inform decided to begin their own secret tests of Compound Q. A year later, the FDA decided to grant its approval to this testing program. As long as the tests were taking place anyway, the FDA said, it at least wanted to know what was going on.[30]

Yet a third change in FDA policy involves the use of parallel tracks in testing programs. In this model, one group of people go through the traditional testing program designed to see if a drug is safe and effective. This track consists of an experimental group and a control group.

A second group of people is simply given the drug and observed for its effects. The idea is that no one really knows whether the new drug will work or not until the test is over. But if it is effective, then people in the second, parallel, group will have had a chance to benefit from it. The FDA refers to the second track in this system as "compassionate" testing.

These changes in FDA policy have started a great debate. Many health authorities believe that the FDA has made some tragic errors in their new policies. For the first time in history, they say, the agency is allowing large numbers of people to have access to untested drugs.[31]

One problem with this policy, they argue, is that some of the untested drugs can be dangerous. Even people who are ill may become sicker or even die as a result of taking drugs the FDA has not yet approved. Some support for that fear developed when two members of the Compound Q test went into comas and died. In this respect, critics say, the FDA has abandoned the very principle upon which it was formed: protecting the health of U.S. citizens.

As two writers on the subject have predicted, the new FDA policies will probably not be limited to AIDS alone. People suffering from other diseases and disorders will expect similar treatment in the future from the nation's watchdog of drug development and approval. But the new FDA practices may make drug use more hazardous for the nation. The writers warn that "consumers and doctors will be forced to make difficult decisions without substantial information at hand."[32]

New FDA policies also threaten the traditional system of drug testing, critics insist. Suppose we select 100 people with AIDS for the formal testing of a new drug. How do we know what other, unapproved drugs those people might be taking? Without knowing that, it is impossible to assess the safety and effectiveness of the drug being tested.

Finally, it may be more difficult to get people with AIDS to take part in trials of new drugs. They may believe that they already have access to "proven"—but not approved—drugs. Why should they take a chance of being in a drug test?

One member of the FDA advisory board put the case this way. The FDA's new policies, he said, say that "anybody can go out and do whatever they want, which is not in the best interests of the people we serve."

Epilogue

In little more than a decade, AIDS has become one of the most difficult problems the world has to deal with. Scientists are working hard to find a cure for the disease and to develop drugs to use against it. Educators are constantly looking for ways to help people avoid becoming infected with HIV.

But, like many diseases, AIDS and HIV infection raise a whole host of questions that go beyond the fields of medicine, science, and education. This book has presented some of these questions: Who should be tested for HIV and what should be done with the test results? How much should government be spending on AIDS research? Should changes be made in the way drugs are tested and released to the public?

Some of these are questions you may have to think about today. How would you feel if *your* school decided to give out condoms to students who asked for them? What is your opinion about students who are HIV positive and attending classes at *your* school?

Other questions will become more important as you grow older. Will you want your family physician to be tested for HIV before she or he delivers your first child? Will *you* want to be tested before undergoing surgery? How do you feel about the cost of AIDS research and care?

These issues are not likely to go away for many years. How will you decide the best way to deal with these issues? Good, reliable, factual information is always the best place to begin. Many people have been hurt and bad social policy has been established simply because people do not know as much about HIV infections as they should or could. Form whatever opinions you like, but always try to base those opinions on the best factual information available.

Perhaps most important, however, are the fundamental beliefs you hold. How should humans treat each other? What obligations does society have toward people who are ill? What responsibility do you *personally* have for friends, neighbors, relatives, and other with who you come into contact? Should people whose lifestyles are different from your own be ignored or punished *because* of those differences?

Only when you really think about some of these fundamental issues of human life will you be able to decide how to deal with the more specific questions outlined in this book. The challenge is a difficult one, but the lives of millions of people will be affected by the decisions that people like yourself make.

Notes by Chapter

Chapter 2

1. As described by the three major television networks. See James Kinsella. *Covering the Plague: AIDS and the American Media* (New Brunswick, NJ: Rutgers University Press, 1989), p. 186.

2. Kinsella, p. 191.

3. For a discussion of public attitudes about the reliability of scientific information, see David F. Musto, "Quarantine and the Problem of AIDS," in Elizabeth Fee and Daniel M. Fox. *AIDS: The Burden of History.* (Berkeley: University of California Press, 1988), p. 83.

4. Kinsella, p. 191.

5. "The Quiet Victories of Ryan White," *People*, May 30, 1988, p. 88.

6. Kinsella, p. 192.

7. As cited in Eric T. Juengst and Barbara A. Koenig. *The Meaning of AIDS.* (New York: Praeger, 1989), p. 142.

8. Victor Gong and Norman Rudnick, eds. *AIDS: Facts and Issues.* (New Brunswick, NJ: Rutgers University Press, 1987), p. 320.

9. *New York Times*, March 28, 1991, p. A1.

Chapter 3

1. Keewhan Choi, "Assembling the AIDS Puzzle: Epidemiology," in Victor Gong and Norman Rudnicks (eds.) *AIDS: Facts and Issues*, (New Bruswick, NJ; Rutgers University Press, 1987), p. 25.

2. This estimate has not changed in about five years. For a discussion of the problems involved in making this estimate, see Joseph Palca, "CDC Abandons Plan for AIDS Survey," *Science*, January 18, 1991, p. 264.

3. Centers for Disease Control, *Morbidity and Mortality Weekly Report*, January 25, 1991, pp. 41–44, and Tedd V. Ellerbrock, Timothy J. Bush, Mary E. Chamberland, and Margaret J. Oxtoby, "Epidemiology of Women With AIDS in the United States, 1981 Through 1990," *JAMA*, June 12, 1991, pp. 2971–2975.

4. Ellerbrock et al., "Epidemiology of Women," p. 2971.

5. *Report of the Presidential Commission on the Human Immunodeficiency Virus Epidemic* (Washington: U.S. Government Printing Office, June 24, 1988), pp. 12–13.

6. Doug Podolsky, "AIDS Strikes Small Towns," *U.S. News & World Report*, December 31, 1990/January 7, 1991, p. 54.

7. Randy Shilts. *And the Band Played On* (New York: St. Martin's Press, 1987), p. 138.

8. The disease is also known as *acquired immune deficiency syndrome*.

9. Dr. Duesberg's position is outlined in "Human Immunodeficiency Virus and Acquired Immunodeficiency Syndrome: Correlation but not Causation," *Proceedings of the National Academy of Science*, February 1989, pp. 755–764.

10 Keay Davidson and Lisa M. Krieger, "Scientist denies HIV causes AIDS," *San Francisco Chronicle*, July 1, 1990, p. D15.

11. One form of *Candida* does cause the most common type of sexually transmitted disease known as candidiasis, monilia, or "yeast."

12. Gayling Gee and Theresa A. Moran. *AIDS: Concepts in Nursing Practice*. (Baltimore: Williams & Wilkins, 1988), p. 33.

13. To be correct the ELISA test should always be described as an HIV *antibody* test. However, it is often referred to in everyday language as simply an "HIV test."

14. "A Candidate's Caveat," *San Francisco Chronicle*, December 17, 1987, p. A8, quoting the Presidential Campaign Hotline of Robertson's meeting with the editorial board of the *Concord Monitor* (NH).

15. Allison L. Greenspan, formerly chief of Information Dissemination Unit, Technical Information Activity, Division of HIV/AIDS (DHA), Center for Infectious Diseases, Centers for Disease Control, personal communication, July 17, 1991.

Chapter 4

1. "HIV Cases Now Estimated At 10 Million," *San Francisco Chronicle*, August 1, 1990, p. A14.

2. David Perlman, "AIDS Changing Course," *San Francisco Chronicle*, June 20, 1990, p. A8. Also see David Talbot "Condom Conundrum," *Mother Jones*, January 1990, pp. 39–46.

3. Stanley Meisler, "Spain's Controversial Condom Giveaway," *Sunday Punch* (of the *San Francisco Examiner*), December 9, 1990, p. 2.

4. Ken Sidey, "AIDS Reshapes Africa's Future," *Christianity Today*, October 22, 1990, p. 47.

5. Hung Fan, Ross F. Conner, and Luis P. Villareal. *The Biology of AIDS*. (Boston: Jones and Bartlett, 1989), p. 138.

6. Peter Aggleton, Graham Hart, and Peter Davies. *AIDS: Social Representations, Social Practices*. (New York: The Falmer Press, 1989), p. 27.

7. "AIDS Forecast Jolts Uganda—Condoms OKd," *San Francisco Chronicle*, February 7, 1991, p. A19.

8. "Grim prediction on AIDS Infection in the Americas," *San Francisco Chronicle*, March 11, 1991, p. A5.

9. Joyce Hackel, "Salvador Prostitutes Hit Hard by AIDS," *San Francisco Examiner*, March 17, 1991, p. A13.

10. Ana Puga, "AIDS Starting to Plague Mexico's Youth," *San Francisco Examiner*, November 19, 1989, p. E7.

11. Bruce Hilton, "Cuba Reports On Lifetime Quarantine," *San Francisco Examiner*, July 8, 1990, p. A6.

12. Scott Hildula, "Increasing Concern Over Brazil's AIDS Epidemic," *San Francisco Chronicle*, March 20, 1991, (Z-1) p. 2.

13. "AIDS Among Women to Double by 2000," *Public Health Reports*, March 1991, p. 216.

14. "AIDS Among Women," p. 216. Also see Antonia C. Novello, "From the Surgeon General, US Public Health Service," *JAMA*, April 10, 1991, p. 1805.

Chapter 5

1. "AFRAIDS," *New Republic*, October 14, 1985, pp. 7–8, reprinted in Robert Emmet Long ed. *AIDS*. (New York: H. W. Wilson, 1987), pp. 133–137.

2. "National News in Brief," *The Advocate*, November 10, 1987, p. 46.

3. "National News in Brief," *The Advocate*, October 27, 1987, p. 24.

4. "National News in Brief," *The Advocate*, September 29, 1987, p. 25.

5. "National News in Brief," *The Advocate*, August 18, 1987, p. 24.

6. Alain L. Sanders, "Fighting AIDS Discrimination" *Time*, September 5, 1988, p. 38.

7. Norma Underwood, "Getting The Message," *MacLean's*, January 1, 1990, pp. 34–36.

8. Gregory M. Herek and Eric K. Glunt, "An Epidemic of Stigma," *American Psychologist*, November 1988, p. 886.

9. Jessica Portner, "Fighting Back," *The Progressive*, August 1990, p. 30.

10. Portner, p. 30.

11. Dennis Altman. *AIDS in the Mind of America* (Garden City, N.Y.: Anchor Books, 1987), p. 60.

12. Altman, p. 60.

13. "National News in Brief," *The Advocate*, September 15, 1987, p. 27.

14. A valuable reference for cases like these is *The Advocate*, a national magazine for gay men and lesbians.

15. David E. Rogers and Eli Ginzberg. *Public and Professional Attitudes toward AIDS Patients* (Boulder, CO: Westview Press, 1989), pp. 20–23.

16. For a specific example, see the proposal of Houston mayoral candidate Louie Welch to solve the AIDS epidemic by "Shooting All The Queers," in the *Dallas Times Herald*, October 20, 1985, p. 1, as quoted in Arthur Frederick Ide. *AIDS Hysteria*. 2nd ed. (Dallas: Monument Press, 1988), p. 65.

17. See, for example, Randy Shilts. *And the Band Played On* (New York: St. Martin's Press, 1987); James Kinsella. *Covering the Plague: AIDS and the American Media* (New Brunswick, NJ: Rutgers University Press, 1989), pp. 259-270; Rogers and Ginzberg. p. 92; Peter Aggleton, Graham Hart, and Peter Davies. *AIDS: Social Representations, Social Practices*, ch. 1, (New York: Falmer Press, 1989); and Victor Gong and Norman Rudnick, eds. *AIDS: Facts and Issues* ch. 15, (New Brunswick, NJ: Rutgers University Press, 1987).

18. As quoted in *Newsweek*, August 12, 1985, in Eric T. Juengst and Barbara A. Koenig. *The Meaning of AIDS* (New York: Praeger, 1989), p. 32.

19. Susan Yoachum, "Buchanan Calls AIDS 'Retribution'," *San Francisco Chronicle*, February 28, 1992, p. A1.

20. Terry Muck, "AIDS: Evangelical Attitudes,"*Christianity Today*, November 18, 1988, p. 15.

21. Kinsella, p. 3.

22. Kinsella, p. 266.

23. Kinsella, p. 2.

24. See Harold Edgar and David J. Rothman, "New Rules for New Drugs," in Dorothy Nelkin, David P. Willis, and Scott V. Parris, eds. *A Disease of Society* (Cambridge: Cambridge University Press, 1991), p. 95.

25. Rogers and Ginzberg, p. 48; also see studies reported in Rogers and Ginzberg, pp. 31-32.

26. Martin Gunderson, David J. Mayo, and Frank S. Rhame. *AIDS: Testing and Privacy*. (Salt Lake City: University of Utah Press, 1989), pp. 199–200.

27. These arguments and rebuttals are summarized in Gunderson, Mayo, and Rhame, pp. 192–203.

28. William F. Buckley, "Crucial Steps in Combatting the AIDS Epidemic: Identify All The Carriers," *New York Times*, March 18, 1986, p. A27.

29. David Perlman, "New Push to Require AIDS Tests," *San Francisco Chronicle*, May 29, 1991, p. A10.

30. See, for example, the analysis in Gunderson, Mayo, and Rhame. pp. 38–41, 155–158, and 192–193.

31. Gunderson, Mayo, and Rhame, pp. 192–193.

32. I thank Rev. Margaret R. Reinfeld, director of education at Gay Men's Health Crisis, New York City, for pointing out this observation.

Chapter 6

1. Barbara A. Misztal, and David Moss, eds. *Action on AIDS* (New York: Greenwood Press, 1990), pp. 31–32.

2. Larry Katzenstein, "When He Has AIDS—And She Doesn't Know," *American Health*, January/February 1991, p. 62.

3. Thomas B. Stoddard and Walter Rieman, "AIDS and the Rights of the Individual," in Dorothy Nelkin, David P. Willis, and Scott V. Parris, eds. *A Disease of Society* (Cambridge: Cambridge University Press, 1991), p. 266.

4. David Perlman, "New Push to Require AIDS Tests," *San Francisco Chronicle*, May 29, 1991, p. A10.

5. Christopher Monckton, "AIDS: A British View," *American Spectator*, January 1987, pp. 29–32.

6. Ronald Bayer. *Private Acts, Social Consequences* (New York: Free Press, 1989), p. 169.

7. "AIDS: What Is To Be Done?" *Harper's*, October 1985, pp. 39-52, as reprinted in Robert Emmet Long, ed. *AIDS* (New York: H. W. Wilson, 1987), p. 175.

8. Michael Quam and Nancy Ford, "AIDS Policies and Practices in the United States," in Misztal and Moss, *Action on AIDS*, pp. 32-33.

9. M. Mills, C. B. Wofsy, and J. Mills, "The Acquired Immunodeficiency Syndrome: Infection Control and Public Health Law," *New England Journal of Medicine*, April 3, 1986, pp. 931–936.

10. Bayer, p. 169.

11. David F. Musto, "Quarantine and the Problem of AIDS," in Elizabeth Fee and Daniel M. Fox. *AIDS: The Burden of History* (Berkeley: University of California Press, 1988), pp. 67–85.

12. See Stoddard and Rieman, "AIDS and the Rights of the Individual," in Nelkin, Willis, and Parris, *A Disease of Society*, pp. 241–271.

13. W. F. Buckley, Jr., "Crucial Steps in Combatting the AIDS Epidemic: Identify All the Carriers," *New York Times*, March 18, 1986, p. A27.

14. "AIDS Needs Medical, Not Emotional, Solutions," letters to the *New York Times*, March 27, 1986, p. A26.

15. David E. Rogers and Eli Ginzberg. *Public and Professional Attitudes toward AIDS Patients* (Boulder, CO: Westview Press, 1989), pp. 34–35.

16. *Report of the Presidential Commission on the Human Immunodeficiency Virus Epidemic* (Washington: U.S. Government Printing Office, June 1988), p. 76.

17. Martin Gunderson, David J. Mayo, and Frank S. Rhame. *AIDS: Testing and Privacy* (Salt Lake City: University of Utah Press, 1989), p. 213.

18. Gunderson, Mayo, and Rhame, p. 214.

19. Gunderson, Mayo, and Rhame, p. 165.

20. Eric T. Juengst and Barbara A. Koenig. *The Meaning of AIDS* (New York: Praeger, 1989), p. 170.

21. "High Risks," *Forbes*, April 25, 1988, p. 130.

22. "Truth In Insurance," *Fortune*, September 26, 1988, p. 210.

23. Jill Eden, Laurie Mount, and Lawrence Miike, *AIDS and Health Insurance*. (Washington, DC: Office of Technology Assessment, 1988), pp. 42–43.

24. Eden, Mount, and Miike, p. 12.

25. Juengst and Koenig, p. 170.

26. David Tuller, "Suit Assails Insurer For Canceling Policy," *San Francisco Chronicle*, May 26, 1990, p. A4.

27. See, for example, Susan B. Garland, "Sure, You Can Get Sick—But Not Too Sick," *Business Week*, December 3, 1990, p. 40; Joan O'C Hamilton, "Insurers Pass The Buck On AIDS Patients," *Business Week*, March 28, 1988, p. 27; and Joan O'C Hamilton, "AIDS: Where Insurers Are Showing Little Mercy," *Business Week*, November 21, 1988, pp. 86–87.

28. Juengst and Koenig, p.170.

29. "Health Insurance Now Available for Persons with AIDS," *San Francisco Bay Times*, March 1991, p. 20.

30 . "Report of the Presidential Commission on the Human Immunodeficiency Virus Epidemic," p. XIX.

31. Sheldon H. Landesman, Howard L. Minkoff, and Anne Willoughby, "HIV Disease in Reproductive Age Women: A Problem of the Present," *JAMA*, March 3, 1989, pp. 1326–1327.

32. Harry W. Haverkos and Robert Edelman, "The Epidemiology of Acquired Immunodeficiency Syndrome Among Heterosexuals," *JAMA*, October 7, 1988, p. 1927.

33. "The Suitability of HIV-positive Individuals for Marriage and Pregnancy," *JAMA*, February 17, 1989, p. 933.

34. Ronald Bayer. "AIDS and the Future of Reproductive Freedom," in Nelkin, Willis, and Parris, *A Disease of Society*, p. 195.

35. Bayer, pp. 201–205.

36. Donald p. Francis and James Chin, "The Prevention of Acquired Immunodeficiency Syndrome in the United States," *JAMA*, March 13, 1987, p. 1360.

37. "The Suitability of HIV-positive Individuals," p. 993.

38. George Annas, "Protecting the Liberty of Pregnant Patients," *New England Journal of Medicine*, May 7, 1987, p. 1213.

39. Philip J. Hilts, "In Shift, Health Chief Lifts Ban on Visitors With the AIDS Virus," *New York Times*, January 4, 1991, p. A15.

40. Hilts, p. A15.

41. Karen De Witt, "U.S., in Switch, Plans to Keep Out People Infected With AIDS Virus," *New York Times*, May 26, 1991, p. L1.

42. De Witt, p. L1.

43. De Witt, p. L15.

Chapter 7

1. D.K. Henderson, "AIDS and the Health-Care Worker: Management of Human Immunodeficiency Virus Infection in the Health-Care Setting," *AIDS Updates*, September/October 1988, pp. 1-12, as reported in Sue Perdew. *Facts about AIDS: A Guide for Health Care Providers* (Philadelphia: Lippincott, 1990), p. 25.

2. Sam B. Puckett and Alan R. Emery. *Managing AIDS in the Workplace* (Reading, MA: Addison-Wesley, 1988), p. 37.

3. Allison L. Greenspan, former chief of Information Dissemination Unit, Technical Information Activity, Division of HIV/AIDS (DHA), Center for Infectious Diseases, Centers for Disease Control, personal communication, July 17, 1991.

4. See Debra Ann Oliver, "AIDS, Universal Precautions, and the Elderly," *RN*, June 1991, pp. 77–78.

5. Perdew, *Facts about AIDS*, p. 25.

6. "Young Doctors Say They Fear AIDS," *San Francisco Chronicle*, January 1, 1991, p. A4.

7. Elaine Herscher, "AIDS Risks Faced by UCSF Interns," *San Francisco Chronicle*, January 24, 1991, p. A2.

8. "4 S.F. Nurses File Suit Over Hospital A.I.D.S. Ward Policies," *San Francisco Chronicle*, August 16, 1985, p. A1.

9. Carroll, Jerry, "The Doctor Who's Afraid of Blood," *San Francisco Chronicle*, November 13, 1989, p. B4.

10. Carroll, p. B4.

11. "Illinois Governor Signs AIDS Notification Law," *San Francisco Chronicle*, October 5, 1991, p. A8.

12. David E. Rogers and Eli Ginzberg. *Public and Professional Attitudes Toward AIDS Patients*, (Boulder, CO: Westview Press, 1989), p. 31.

13. Rogers and Ginzberg, p. 25.

14. Hilton, Bruce, "When Doctors Walk Out On The Job," *San Francisco Chronicle*, March 11, 1990, p. D18.

15. As quoted in *Report of the Presidential Commission on the Human Immunodeficiency Virus Epidemic*, (Washington, D.C.: U.S. Government Printing Office, 1988), p. 137.

16. Jayne Garrison, "AIDS and the Health Care Worker," *San Francisco Chronicle*, January 27, 1991, p. D14.

17. "The Odds of Getting HIV if Your Doctor Has It," *San Francisco Chronicle*, February 7, 1991, p. A7.

18. David Tuller and Elaine Herscher, "Debate on Medical Workers With HIV," *San Francisco Chronicle*, February 20, 1991, p. A10.

19. Tuller and Herscher, p. A10.

20. Garrison, p. D14.

Chapter 8

1. Charles F. Turner, Heather G. Miller, and Lincoln E. Moses, eds. *AIDS: Sexual Behavior and Intravenous Drug Use* (Washington, DC: National Academy Press, 1989), pp. 20 and 376–378.

2. Office of Technology Assessment. *Review of the Public Health Service's Response to AIDS* (Washington, DC: Office of Technology Assessment, 1985), p. 53.

3. National Academy of Science—Institute of Medicine. *Confronting AIDS* (Washington, DC: Academy Press, 1986), p.97.

4. *New York Times*, April 29, 1988, p. B4, as reported in Ronald Bayer. *Private Acts, Social Consequences* (New York: The Free Press, 1989), p. 218.

5. "National News in Brief, "*The Advocate*, November 24, 1987, p. 15.

6. Department of Health and Human Services; Public Health Service. *Surgeon General's Report on Acquired Immune Deficiency Syndrome* (Washington, DC: Department of Health and Human Services, 1987), p. 4.

7. *Surgeon General's Report*, p. 31.

8. As cited in Bayer, p. 216.

9. See Turner, Miller, and Moses, pp. 383–385.

10. "National News in Brief," *The Advocate*, November 10, 1987, p. 39.

11. "National News in Brief," *The Advocate*, July 5, 1988, p. 16.

12. "National News in Brief," *The Advocate*, November 8, 1988, p. 22.

13. David E. Rogers and Eli Ginzberg. *Public and Professional Attitudes toward AIDS Patients* (Boulder, CO: Westview Press, 1989), p. 24.

14. See Edgar and Rothman in Nelkin, Willis, and Parris, especially pp. 95–97.

15. Marlene Cimons, "Resentment Over Special Status of AIDS in Health Financing," *San Francisco Chronicle*, June 21, 1990, p. A13.

16. See, for example, Pete Hamill, "Confessions of a Heterosexual," *Esquire*, August 1990, pp. 55–57 and Chris Adams, "Wild In The Streets," *Image Magazine* (of the *San Francisco Examiner*), June 17, 1990, pp. 15–19.

17. William B. Johnston and Kevin R. Hopkins. *The Catastrophe Ahead* (New York: Praeger, 1990), p. 45.

18. Hard data to support this view are not readily available, however. See Turner, Miller, and Moses, pp. 215–217 and 230-231.

19. Elaine Herscher, "Coalition Urges Needle Exchange in San Francisco," *San Francisco Chronicle*, September 12, 1989, p. A2.

20. Lori Olszewski, "Needle Swaps Denounced," *San Francisco Chronicle*, May 17, 1989, p. A24.

21. "S.F. Mayor Cancels Plans To Protect Addicts From A.I.D.S.," *San Francisco Chronicle*, July 26, 1986, p. A2.

22. See, for example, *American Journal of Public Health*, October 1989, pp. 1355-1357, and Richard C. Stephens, Thomas E. Feucht, and Shadi W. Roman, "Effects of an Intervention Program on AIDS-related Drug and Needle Behavior Among Intravenous Drug Users, *American Journal of Public Health*, May 1991, pp. 568-571.

23. William Booth, "Sullivan Opposes Needle-Exchange Programs," *Washington Post*, July 20, 1989, p. A3.

24. "AIDS: Public Attitudes and Education Needs," Roper poll for Gay Mens' Health Crisis (n.d., [ca. 1991]), p. 35.

25. Herscher, p. A2.

26. Turner, Miller, and Moses, pp. 383–385.

27. "N.Y. City Students Will Be Offered Condoms at School," *San Francisco Chronicle*, February 28, 1991, p. A19.

28. See the discussion of this issue in the *New York Times*, December 5, 1990, p. B3 and December 6, 1990, p. B1.

29. "Key institutions back condoms for N.Y. students," *San Francisco Examiner*, March 17, 1991, p. A8.

30. "Living with HIV," (San Francisco: Impact AIDS, 1990), p. 2.

31. Wendy Chavkin, et al., "Women and AIDS," *Science*, January 25, 1991, p. 359.

32. Rozanne Brown, "AIDS: The Growing Threat To Black Heterosexuals," *Ebony*, January 1991, p. 86. Also see P. Orenstein, "Women at Risk," *Vogue*, November 1990, pp. 370–371.

33. *Living with HIV*, p. 2.

34. See, for example, the discussion in Brown.

35. Karen Hein, "Fighting AIDS in Adolescents," *Issues in Science and Technology*, Spring 1991, p. 69.

36. Turner, Miller, and Moses, p. 304.

37. Turner, Miller, and Moses, p. 305.

38. Turner, Miller, and Moses, p. 305.

39. Pia Hinckle, "Counselors Plead for More Help For Young People With AIDS," *San Francisco Chronicle*, June 18, 1991, p. A4.

Chapter 9

1. Dennis Altman. *AIDS in the Mind of America* (Garden City, NY: Anchor Books, 1987), pp. 113 and 208.

2. Altman, p. 112.

3. Altman, p. 112.

4. Altman, p. 112.

5. James Kinsella. *Covering the Plague: AIDS and the American Media* (New Brunswick, NJ: Rutgers University Press, 1989), p. 180.

6. Ibid. p.180.

7. Naomi, Freundlich, "No, Spending More On AIDS Isn't Unfair," *Business Week*, September 17, 1990, p. 37.

8. Altman, p. 47.

9. James J. Kilpatrick, "Aren't We Overreacting to AIDS?" *Washington Post*, June 9, 1988, as quoted in William B. Johnston, and Kevin R. Hopkins. *The Catastrophe Ahead.* (New York: Praeger, 1990), p. 59.

10. Charles Krauthammer, "AIDS: Getting More Than Its Share?" *Time*, June 25, 1990, p. 80.

11. Michael Fumento. *The Myth of Heterosexual AIDS* (New York: Basic Books, 1990), Ch. 21.

12. Michael Fumento, "Are We Spending Too Much on AIDS?" *Commentary*, October 1990, pp. 51-53.

13. Fumento, p. 51

14. Fumento, p. 51.

15. Freundlich, p. 37.

16. Fumento, "Are We Spending Too Much on AIDS?" p. 52.

17. "U.S. Agency's Response to AIDS Crisis Praised," *San Francisco Chronicle*, March 8, 1991, p. A11.

18. Freundlich, p. 37. Also see Charles F. Turner, Heather G. Miller, and Lincoln E. Moses, eds. *AIDS.: Sexual Behavior and Intravenous Drug Use* (Washington, DC: National Academy Press, 1989). pp. 447–449.

19. Freundlich, p. 37.

20. Freundlich, p. 37.

21. Freundlich, p. 37.

22. Fumento, "Are We Spending Too Much on AIDS?" p. 51.

23. Fumento, p. 52.

24. Fumento, p. 52.

25. David Shaw, "The Epidemic: Did The Press Cry Wolf?" *New York Times Book Review*, January 7, 1990, p. 7.

26. James E. Van Buskirk, *Library Journal*, November 15, 1989, p. 99, and Larry Bush and Ralph de Vere White, "The Myth Of The Myth: Two Responses," *San Francisco Review of Books*, Winter 1989, p. 6.

27. David E. Rogers, and Eli Ginzberg. *Public and Professional Attitudes toward AIDS Patients* (Boulder, CO: Westview Press, 1989), p. 106.

28. *AIDS Treatment News* is available from ATN Publications, P.O. Box 411256, San Francisco, CA 94141.

29. For a statement of this argument, see Denise Grady, " 'Look, Doctor, I'm Dying. Give Me the Drug,' " *Discover*, August 1986, pp. 78-86.

30. David Tuller, " 'Renegade' Tests Of AIDS Drug Get FDA Sanction," *San Francisco Chronicle*, March 9, 1990, p. A1.

31. For a discussion of these changes, see Harold Edgar and David J. Rothman, "New Rules for New Drugs," in Dorothy Nelkin, David P. Willis, and Scott V. Parris. *A Disease of Society*, (Cambridge: Cambridge University Press, 1991), pp. 84–115.

32. Edgar and Rothman, p. 112.

Further Reading

Altman, Dennis. *AIDS in the Mind of America*. Garden City, NY: Anchor Books, 1987.

Aggleton, Peter, Graham Hart, and Peter Davies. *AIDS: Social Representations, Social Practices*. New York: The Falmer Press, 1989.

Bayer, Ronald. *Private Acts, Social Consequences*. New York: The Free Press, 1989.

Brown, Roxanne. "AIDS: The Growing Threat to Black Heterosexuals." *Ebony*, January 1991, pp. 84 +.

Eden, Jill, Laurie Mount, and Lawrence Miike. *AIDS and Health Insurance*. Washington, D.C.: Office of Technology Assessment, 1988.

Fan, Hung, Ross F. Conner, and Luis P. Villareal. *The Biology of AIDS*. Boston: Jones and Bartlett, 1989.

Fee, Elizabeth, and Daniel M. Fox. *AIDS: The Burden of History*. Berkeley, Calif.: University of California Press, 1988.

Fleming, Alan F., et al., eds. *The Global Impact of AIDS*. New York: Alan R. Liss, Inc., 1988.

Flygare, Thomas J. "Judge Orders Children with AIDS Virus Back Into the Classroom." *Phi Delta Kappan*, January 1988, pp. 381–382.

Freundlich, Naomi. "No, Spending More On AIDS Isn't Unfair." *Business Week*, September 17, 1990, p. 37.

Fumento, Michael. "Are We Spending Too Much on AIDS?" *Commentary*, October 1990, pp. 51–53.

———. *The Myth of Heterosexual AIDS*. New York: Basic Books, 1990.

Gee, Gayling and Theresa A. Moran, eds. *AIDS: Concepts in Nursing Practice*. Baltimore: Williams & Wilkins, 1988.

Gillepsie, Marcia Ann. "Women and AIDS." *Ms.*, January 2, 1991, pp. 16–22.

Gong, Victor, and Norman Rudnick, eds. *AIDS: Facts and Issues*. New Brunswick, N.J.: Rutgers University Press, 1987.

Goodman, David. "Door Knocking for AIDS." *Technology Review*, May/June 1988, pp. 10-11.

Gunderson, Martin, David J. Mayo, and Frank S. Rhame. *AIDS: Testing and Privacy*. Salt Lake City: University of Utah Press, 1989.

Hamilton, Joan, O'C. "AIDS: Where Insurers Are Showing Little Mercy." *Business Week*, November 21, 1988, pp. 86–87.

———. "Insurers Pass the Buck on AIDS Patients." *Business Week*, March 28, 1988, p. 27.

Hein, Karen. "Fighting AIDS in Adolescents." *Issues in Science and Technology*, Spring 1991, pp. 67–72.

Herek, Gregory M., and Eric K. Glunt. "An Epidemic of Stigma." *American Psychologist*, November 1988, pp. 886–891.

Institute of Medicine, National Academy of Sciences. *Confronting AIDS: Directions for Public Health, Health Care, and Research*. Washington, D.C.: National Academy Press, 1986.

Johnston, William B., and Kevin R. Hopkins. *The Catastrophe Ahead*. New York: Praeger, 1990.

Juengst, Eric T., and Barbara A. Koenig. *The Meaning of AIDS*. New York: Praeger, 1989.

Kelly, Jeffrey A., et al. "Stigmatization of AIDS Patients by Physicians." *American Journal of Public Health*, July 1987, pp. 789–791.

Keough, Katherine E., and George Seaton. "Superintendents' Views on AIDS: A National Survey." *Phi Delta Kappan*, January 1988, pp. 358–361.

Kinsella, James. *Covering the Plague: AIDS and the American Media.* New Brunswick, N.J.: Rutgers University Press, 1989.

Kowalewski, Mark R. "Religious Constructions of the AIDS Crisis" *Sociological Analysis*, Spring 1990, pp. 91–96.

Krauthammer, Charles "AIDS: Getting More Than Its Share?" *Time*, June 25, 1990, p. 80.

Leukefeld, C. G., R. J. Battjest, and Z. Amsel. *AIDS and Intravenous Drug Use: Future Directions for Community-Based Prevention Research.* Washington, D.C.: U.S. Department of Health and Human Services, Public Health Service, National Institute on Drug Abuse, 1990.

Long, Robert Emmet, ed. *AIDS.* New York: The H. W. Wilson Company, 1987.

Misztal, Barbara A., and David Moss, eds. *Action on AIDS.* New York: Greenwood Press, 1990.

Murphy, Timothy F. "No Time for AIDS Backlash." *Hastings Center Report*, March/April 1991, pp. 7-11.

Nelkin, Dorothy, David P. Willis, and Scott V. Parris, eds. *A Disease of Society.* Cambridge: Cambridge University Press, 1991.

Nelson, James B. "Responding To, Learning From AIDS." *Christianity and Crisis*, May 19, 1986, pp. 176–181.

Novick, Alvin. "Civil Disobedience in The Time of AIDS." *Hastings Center Report*, November/December 1989, pp. 35–36.

Office of Technology Assessment. *Review of the Public Health Service's Response to AIDS.* Washington, DC: Office of Technology Assessment, 1985.

Perdew, Sue. *Facts About AIDS: A Guide for Health Care Providers.* Philadelphia: J. B. Lippincott, 1990.

Plant, Martin A. *AIDS, Drugs, and Prostitution*. London: Tavistock /Routledge, 1990.

Portner, Jessica. "Fighting Back." *The Progressive*, August 1990, pp. 30–32.

Puckett, Sam B., and Alan R. Emery. *Managing AIDS in the Workplace*. Reading, Mass.: Addison-Wesley, 1988.

Queenan, Joe. "Straight Talk About AIDS." *Forbes*, June 26, 1989, pp. 41–42.

"The Quiet Victories of Ryan White." *People Magazine*, May 30, 1988, pp. 88–90.

"Report of the Presidential Commission on the Human Immunodeficiency Virus Epidemic" Washington, D.C.: U.S. Government Printing Office, June 24, 1988.

Sanders, Alain L. "Fighting AIDS Discrimination." *Time*, September 5, 1988, p. 38.

Shilts, Randy. *And the Band Played On*. New York: St. Martin's Press, 1987.

Spiers, Herbert R. "AIDS and Civil Disobedience." *Hastings Center Report*, November/December 1989, pp. 34–35.

Turner, Charles F., Heather G. Miller, and Lincoln E. Moses, eds. *AIDS, Sexual Behavior and Intravenous Drug Use*. Washington, D.C.: National Academy Press, 1989.

Whitman, David. "Inside an AIDS Colony." *U.S. News & World Report*, January 29, 1990, pp. 20–26.

INDEX